A · C · S · I

BIBLE

GRADE TWO

Acknowledgements

ACSI President — Dr. Ken Smitherman

ACSI Executive Vice-President — Mr. James F. Burdick

ACSI Vice-President for Academic Affairs — Dr. Derek Keenan

ACSI Director of Curriculum/Managing Editor — Dr. Sharon R. Berry

Assistant Editors
Mrs. Mary Jo Kynerd, Birmingham, AL
Miss Renee Pate, Birmingham, AL
Dr. Bette Talley, Birmingham, AL

Authors
Mrs. Barbara Alexander, Aurora, IL
Mrs. Linda Causey, Birmingham, AL
Mrs. Jan Gillette, Madison Heights, VA
Mrs. Laure Herlinger, Milwaukee, WI
Mrs. Marilyn Phillips, Sacramento, CA
Miss Cheri Schoenrock, Issaquah, WA
Mrs. Darlene Troxel, Rowlett, TX
Mrs. Connie Williams, Bakersfield, CA

Resource Authors
Mrs. Mary Lou Carney, Chesterton, IN
Mrs. Kersten Hamilton, Albuquerque, NM
Mrs. Elizabeth Renicks, Tuscaloosa, AL
Mrs. Karen Stimer, Colorado Springs, CO

Graphic Design and Production
GrowthMasters Corporation
Colorado Springs, CO
Andrew Stimer, President

Project Manager — Karen Stimer

Designers
Chuck Haas
Bill Thielker

Production Coordinator — Charles Morse

Production Artists
Craig Clear
Tim Jaycox
Pat Reinheimer

Production Assistant — Linda Pue

Illustrators
Ron Adair
Barbara Crowe
Alan Flinn
Eric Johnson
Mike Johnson
Cedric Taylor
Linda Wood
Yakovetic Productions

Photographer — Ron Nickel

Table of Contents

Association of Christian Schools International
731 Chapel Hills Drive
Colorado Springs, CO 80920-1027

Welcome to Second Grade Bible!
Are you ready to learn God's Word together?

This year we are going to look at different people in the Bible who can help us. They show us what God wants us to be like. Some of these people were strong and brave. They led armies and fought battles for God. Some of them were famous and traveled all over their world. Some of them wrote parts of the Bible. But all of them show us how we can love and serve God. They will be our heroes.

Some other people will be with us this year too. The Johnsons are missionaries. They will be going to Guatemala to tell people there about the Lord. Mr. Johnson is a preacher. Mrs. Johnson is a mommy and a teacher. Timmy and Tina are just your age – and they're twins! They will be learning many new things in their missionary adventures, and so will you.

Are you ready to study our first Bible character?
Let's see what God shows us about him.

Moses' Life. What do you know about Moses' life? Draw a line from the picture to show when the event happened to Moses.

When he was **young**.

When he was a **man**.

When he was God's **leader**.

B **Verse Search.** Moses knew he needed God's help. That is why God used him as a leader. Look up James 4:6 and answer the question below.

Whom does God help?

C **Which Would You Be?** Look at each picture. Decide if the child is being humble or proud. Write the word **humble** near the pictures that show someone being humble. Write the word **proud** if the person is being proud.

D **Whom Do You See?** Check your vision. This is a special eye chart. Follow the directions to answer the question. Color with a red crayon every part that has the letter **p**. Whom did Moses see in the burning bush?

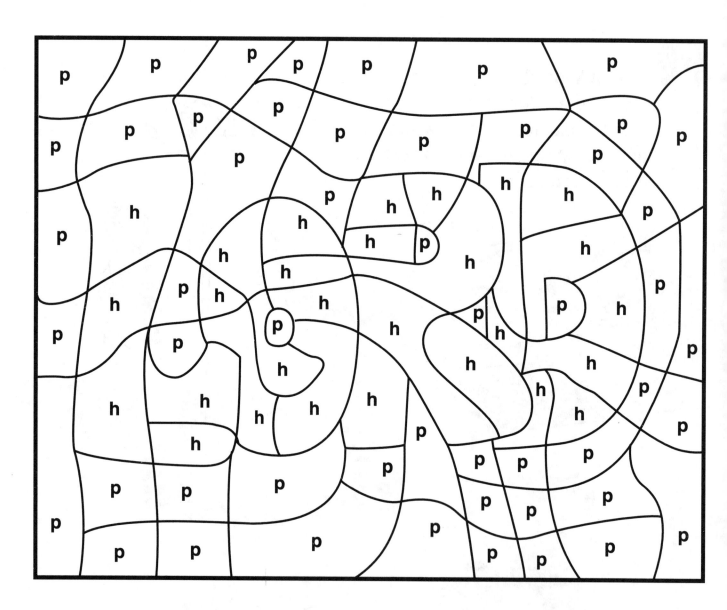

Now check Psalm 25:15a. Where should your eyes always be?

2

A   **Things That Make Me Afraid.** Read the list of things that can make us afraid. Draw a 😞 by the three things that scare you most.

getting lost

bad dreams

storms

admitting when
I'm wrong

going to the dentist

a dark room

being alone

a big dog

snakes, bugs and spiders

taking a test

B **God Answers Moses' Fears.** Moses had been safe and happy in the desert when God called him. He didn't want to go because he was afraid. Three of his fears are listed below. Cut and paste God's answers for his fears.

Moses' Fears:

1. Moses: People won't believe me.

2. Moses: I can't speak well.

3. Moses: Some men want to kill me.

God's Answers:

God: I will help you speak and teach you what to say. (Exodus 4:12)

God: I will do miracles that they may believe. (Exodus 4:8)

God: All the men who wanted to kill you are dead. (Exodus 4:19)

C

Timmy Needs Help. The Johnsons are going to leave next week for the mission field. All Timmy's and Tina's toys have been packed away. Last night they said good-bye to their friends at church. Timmy is thinking about the long trip ahead of him. He doesn't want to leave his room and his baseball team and favorite park. He knows that everything will be strange and different in just a few days. He is afraid that he won't have any friends and that the new school will be very hard. He is even a little afraid of flying in the airplane over the water. What could Timmy do that would help him?

D

Help For Timmy. Write Psalm 56:3. This verse can help Timmy and you.

Psalm 56:3

E **Help For Me.** We have learned this week that God wants His people to have courage. He will help us be courageous when we ask Him. Think of a time when you feel afraid and need some courage. Write a prayer asking God to give you the courage to do what is right.

Dear God,

_____

_____

_____

_____

                                    In Jesus' name,
                                    Amen

F **Check Up.** Take your courage temperature this week. How courageous are you? Circle it.

I do not pray
when I'm afraid.

I sometimes pray
when I'm afraid.

I always pray
when I'm afraid.

A **God Sends the Plagues.** Listen very carefully as your teacher tells the story of Moses and Pharaoh and the ten plagues. As you hear about one of the plagues, find the picture of it below and number it. When you are finished, you will know all about the plagues God sent on Egypt.

_____ frogs

_____ animals die

_____ river turns to blood

_____ hail

_____ darkness

_____ gnats

_____ boils

_____ firstborn sons die

_____ locusts

_____ flies

B **How Many Times?** Make a check mark to show what Pharaoh said to Moses. Then write how many times Pharaoh said "no." _____

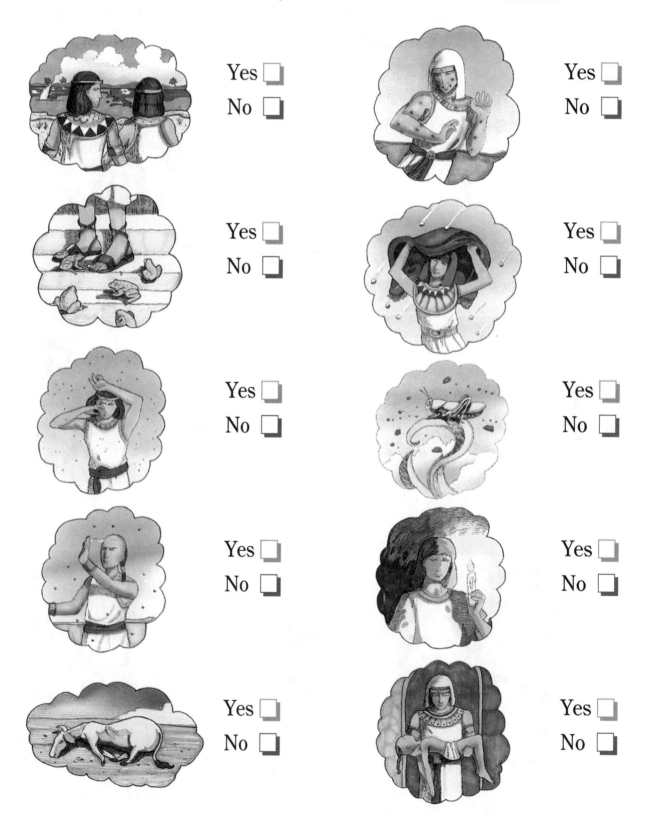

Yes ☐
No ☐

Yes ☐
No ☐

Yes ☐
No ☐

Yes ☐
No ☐

Yes ☐
No ☐

Yes ☐
No ☐

Yes ☐
No ☐

Yes ☐
No ☐

Yes ☐
No ☐

Yes ☐
No ☐

C   **I Can Be Diligent.** Copy the assignments your teacher gives you each day. Then place a big check by each one you finish. Show how diligent you can be. See if you can earn a check by each one.

Day One ★

Day Two ★★

Day Three ☆☆☆

Day Four ★★★★

D **Moses and Pharaoh.** Color the picture, tear it out and hang it up at home to remind you to be diligent.

A **What Was Joshua to Do with God's Word?** List three things God told Joshua to do with the Book of the Law in Joshua 1:8.

1. _____

_____

2. _____

_____

3. _____

_____

B **What Am I to Do with God's Word?** Solve the rebus.

H+ +d      m+

_____ His _____ in _____ _____

t+      m+  +t

_____ _____ _____ sin.

Psalm 119:11

17

C **Finding Your Way Around.** Scene: Three children are at the park. One is sitting, looking through his Bible. The two others come over to him.

Child 1: We'll never find the telephones this way!

Child 2: Sure we will! We'll just keep looking.

Child 1: It would sure be easier if we knew where to look for the signs and what they meant.

Child 2: Hey, there's Billy from school!

Child 1: Hi, Billy! What are you doing?

Billy: I'm looking for a verse in my Bible.

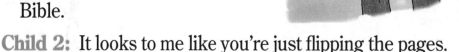

Child 2: It looks to me like you're just flipping the pages.

Billy: Well, I know which verse I'm looking for, but I don't know where it is. There sure are a lot of pages to look through.

Child 1: That's kind of like us, Billy. We're looking for the telephones. We know they are here somewhere, but we never knew this park was so big. We could use some help.

Billy: Oh, that's easy! Just follow this path until you see a sign with a phone and an arrow on it. Follow that sign and you can't miss them!

Child 2: Maybe we could help you, Billy. What verse are you looking for?

Billy: Isaiah 40:8. Unfortunately, I don't know where Isaiah is, and I don't know what those numbers mean.

4

Child 1: Remember when our teacher showed us the Table of Contents in our Bibles? She said there were two parts to our Bibles, an Old Testament in the first part and a New Testament in the last part.

Billy: Yes, I remember that.

Child 1: Well, Isaiah is in the Old Testament part, but close to the end. So it will be about halfway through your Bible.

Child 2: Then the first number tells you which chapter of Isaiah you need to find. All the chapters are numbered with big numbers so you can see them.

Child 1: The number after the two dots is the verse number. So you look at all the verses in chapter 40 until you come to number 8!

Billy: Hey, that's not hard at all!

Child 2: It's as easy as finding your way through the park to the telephones!

Child 1: Yes, especially when you know what the signs mean!

Books of the Old and New Testaments

The Old Testament

	ABBREV.	PAGE			ABBREV.	PAGE
Genesis	Gen.	4		Ecclesiastes	Eccl.	950
Exodus	Ex.	82		Song of Solomon	Song	966
Leviticus	Lev.	146		Isaiah	Is.	978
Numbers	Num.	190		Jeremiah	Jer.	1079
Deuteronomy	Deut.	249		Lamentations	Lam.	1176
Joshua	Josh.	304		Ezekiel	Ezek.	1188
Judges	Judg.	340		Daniel	Dan.	1268
Ruth	Ruth	377		Hosea	Hos.	1295
1 Samuel	1 Sam.	385		Joel	Joel	1313
2 Samuel	2 Sam.	431		Amos	Amos	1322
1 Kings	1 Kin.	472		Obadiah	Obad.	1336
2 Kings	2 Kin.	519		Jonah	Jon.	1339
1 Chronicles	1 Chr.	565		Micah	Mic.	1344
2 Chronicles	2 Chr.	604		Nahum	Nah.	1356
Ezra	Ezra	652		Habakkuk	Hab.	1361
Nehemiah	Neh.	669		Zephaniah	Zeph.	1367
Esther	Esth.	693		Haggai	Hag.	1373
Job	Job	707		Zechariah	Zech.	1377
Psalms	Ps.	762		Malachi	Mal.	1394
Proverbs	Prov.	902				

The New Testament

	ABBREV.	PAGE			ABBREV.	PAGE
Matthew	Matt.	1409		1 Timothy	1 Tim.	1817
Mark	Mark	1472		2 Timothy	2 Tim.	1826
Luke	Luke	1510		Titus	Titus	1834
John	John	1573		Philemon	Philem.	1839
Acts	Acts	1620		Hebrews	Heb.	1842
Romans	Rom.	1680		James	James	1865
1 Corinthians	1 Cor.	1711		1 Peter	1 Pet.	1874
2 Corinthians	2 Cor.	1741		2 Peter	2 Pet.	1884
Galatians	Gal.	1760		1 John	1 John	1890
Ephesians	Eph.	1773		2 John	2 John	1899
Philippians	Phil.	1784		3 John	3 John	1901
Colossians	Col.	1794		Jude	Jude	1903
1 Thessalonians	1 Thess.	1803		Revelation	Rev.	1907
2 Thessalonians	2 Thess.	1811				

D **Who Is Loving God's Word?** Circle each picture which shows someone loving God's Word.

E **What Should I Love?** Use the sentences below to fill in the blank boxes and discover the mystery word in this puzzle. Write the mystery word on the blank line of the sentence at the bottom of the page.

1. Reading God's Word can _____ me.

2. I need to _____ God's Word.

3. God wants me to do my _____ .

4. I _____ God's Word.

5. Read some of God's Word _____ day.

Word Bank

every
best
memorize
bless
love

I should read the _____ every day.

A The Marching Song.

Joshua and his people went
  round and round,
  round and round,
  round and round.
Joshua and his people went
  round and round,
Each of seven days.

The trumpets made a
  loud, loud sound,
  loud, loud sound,
  loud, loud sound.
The trumpets made a
  loud, loud sound,
At the end of each day.

The great big walls fell
  down, down, down,
  down, down, down,
  down, down, down.
The great big walls fell
  down, down, down,
At the end of the seventh day.

B Who Is Following Directions?

Timmy Learns to Obey.

"Timmy, you must sit down in this taxi and keep your hands and head inside the window," said Mrs. Johnson for the second time since getting off the plane in Guatemala.

"I know but there is so much to see and it's too hot!" answered Timmy.

"Timmy, you need to obey your mother. We're concerned for your safety. By the way, what did you two think of the plane ride?" asked Mr. Johnson. "You were very quiet at the end of the flight."

Tina answered, "It was great! I could see the land and water, but...."

"But what, honey?" asked Mrs. Johnson.

Tina answered, "I was feeling sad about not seeing Grandpa and Grandma for a long time...and our friends. I miss them already."

Mr. Johnson said, "We will be able to write letters and call them once in awhile."

Suddenly, Timmy interrupted. "Oh no! My baseball hat!" he yelled. "It's gone! Dad! We have to stop!"

Mr. Johnson said, "Son, what did we tell you?"

Timmy answered sadly, "Sit down and keep my head and hands inside the taxi."

Mr. Johnson continued, "Now do you understand why it's important to do what we tell you?"

"Yes, I do!" replied Timmy. "I'm sorry."

My Family. What are some things that your father or mother asks you to do?

_____

_____

_____

E **Obedience Check.** Ephesians 6:1 tells us that we should obey our parents because it is right. How often do you do what your parents ask you to do? Color the hat that best answers the question. Then write Ephesians 6:1 on the back of the page.

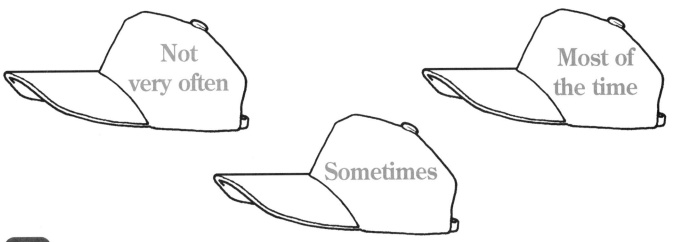

Not very often

Most of the time

Sometimes

F **Marching Order.** Joshua 6:12-13

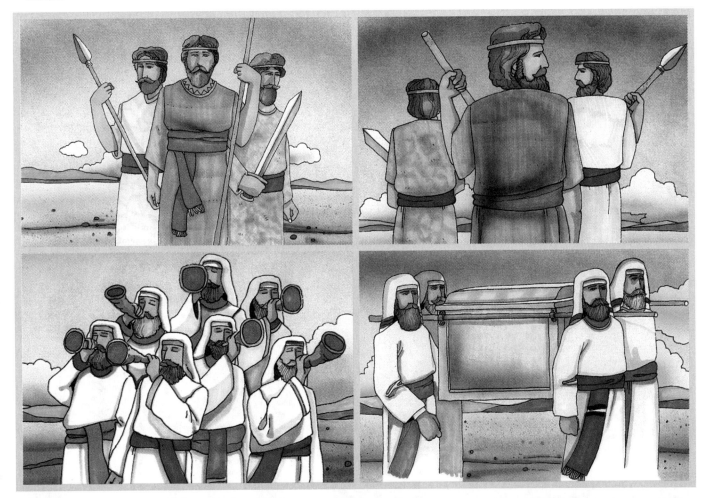

Ephesians 6:1

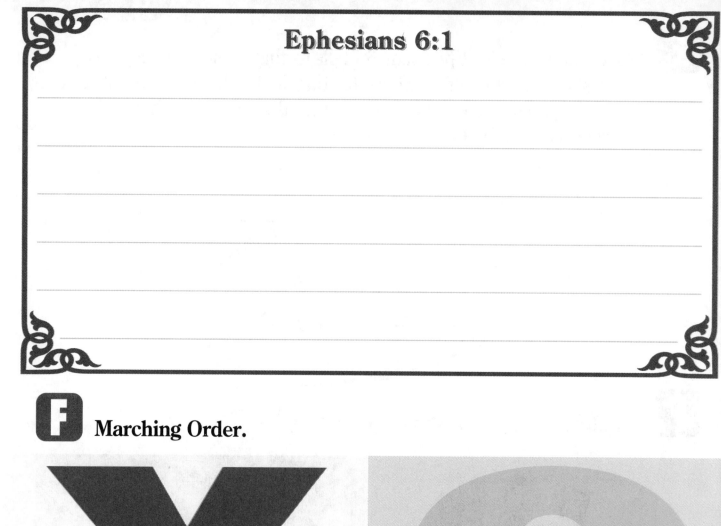

 **Marching Order.**

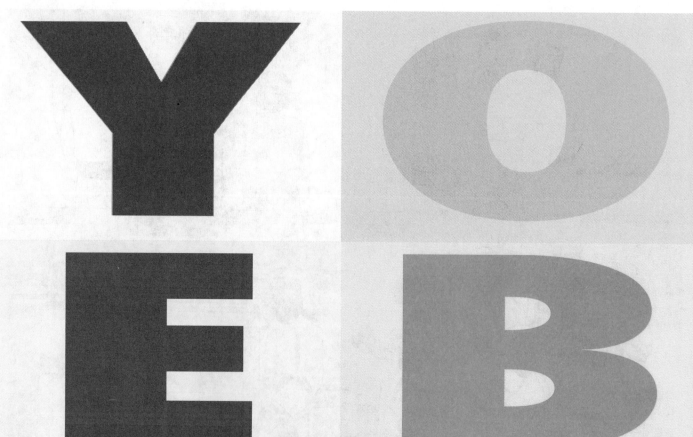

6

A **Temptation Tugs.** As your teacher reads each situation of temptation, decide whether or not this is a temptation for you. Draw a smiling face in the box if you are not usually tempted by this. Draw a frowning face in the box if you are often tempted by this.

1.   4.
2.   5.
3.   6.

B **How to Say "No" to Wrong.** Look up the verses below and draw a line to match the phrase to the verse.

Psalm 119:11

James 4:7b

Joshua 24:15

Just say "No" to evil.

Just say "Yes" to God.

Learn God's Word.

C **Do You Remember?** Complete each of the four commands Joshua gave to the Israelites. Use Joshua 24:14-15 to help you.

1. _____ the Lord.

2. _____ Him.

3. _____ away the false gods.

4. _____ this day whom you will serve.

D **Following God.** Find Mark 12:30 to help you complete the sentences.

Mark 12:30

Love the Lord your God with all your _____, with all your

_____, with all your _____, and with all

your _____.

E **Why Is Heidi Talking to God?** Color this picture while you think about the question.

God's help is always available to us.

F **How Is Your Heart for God?** Joshua was a good leader because he followed God with his whole heart. He chose to love and serve Him every day. Circle the hearts below that are true about you.

I am saying "No" to sin.

I am saying "Yes" to God.

It's hard for me to say "No" to sin.

I am learning God's Word.

It's hard for me to say "Yes" to God.

I don't know what God's Word says about sin.

G **Promises.** Making a promise and keeping it are very important, especially when it is made to God. Write a promise about following God with your whole heart. Cut out the rock shape and attach it to a real rock.

A **What Did Daniel Do?** Use the scrambled letters to finish the poem.

When Daniel faced a problem,

He was not the least afraid;

He placed his trust in God alone,

And confidently _____!

B **Daniel and the King's Bad Dream.** Many people tried to help the king understand his dream. Match each person with the right statement by writing the letter on the blank.

 **a.** Daniel and his three friends

 **b.** King Nebuchadnezzar

 **c.** the king's wise men

 **d.** Daniel

☐ 1. He had a dream he couldn't understand.

☐ 2. They couldn't tell the king what he wanted to know.

☐ 3. He told the king that God knew what he needed.

☐ 4. They asked God for wisdom.

C **Daniel's Secret.** Locate Daniel 2:20 and 23. Daniel was strong and confident because he knew God was able to help him.

What two things did Daniel say belonged to God? (v. 20)

_____   _____

What did God give Daniel in answer to his prayer? (v. 23)

_____   _____

D **What Is God Like?** Think of a word that could be used to describe God. Write the word below. Be creative. Exchange books with a friend and write your word in his or her book. Then color the shapes.

_____   _____

7

E **I Can Pray Like Daniel.** Complete each blank.

1. Write one thing you want to thank God for.

_____

_____

2. Write one thing you want to ask God for.

_____

_____

F **How Does God Feel When I Pray?** "… but the prayer of the upright is His delight." *(Proverbs 15:8)* Use your brightest crayons to color the letters.

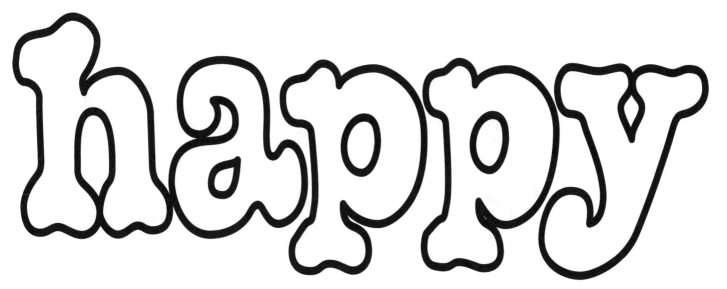

G **I Can Be Confident in God.**

God knew all about me before I was born.
I can be confident in God.

God is my Shepherd and He will care for me by providing for my needs.
I can be confident in God.

God knows when I am asleep and when I am awake.
I can be confident in God.

God knows when I am afraid.
I can be confident in God.

God knows _____.
I can be confident in God.

H **Prayer Check.** We can pray anywhere – at home, at school or at church. We can pray anytime – morning, noon or night. Put a check in the boxes that are true for you.

☐ Last night I prayed before I went to bed.

☐ Today, I prayed at meal time.

A **Stranger in a Strange Land.** Daniel saw many new things in Babylon. Circle the words that best answer the questions.

1. What would have been new and different to Daniel?

food   the sky   money

names   prayer   books

language   people   buildings

animals   clothes   God

2. How do you think Daniel felt in this new place?

happy   lonely   excited

scared   homesick   sleepy   sad

B **The Bible's Record of Faithfulness.** Look up the verses below. Decide if the persons were faithful or unfaithful to God. Place an **X** in the correct box.

Faithful   **Unfaithful**

1. Moses followed God's directions and went to Egypt. (Exodus 4:19-20)

2. The steward wisely used his five talents. (Matthew 25:19-21)

3. The steward with one talent decided to bury it. (Matthew 25:24-28)

4. The widow offered her only two coins. (Mark 12:41-44)

5. Peter and the Apostles determined to obey God by preaching about Jesus. (Acts 5:29)

C **Making a Choice.** Daniel and his friends carefully chose good things to put in their minds and bodies. Circle the good choices you can make.

Bible

bad words

lots of junk food

lots of exercise

my teacher's lessons

jokes that hurt others

watching T.V. many hours

plenty of fruits and vegetables

my parents' teaching

plenty of sleep

D **New Words for Timmy and Tina.**

These are some of the new words we are learning since we arrived here.

Hi!

Hello.................. hola ....(ō′ lä)
Please .... por favor ....(pōr fä vōr′)
Good-bye .... adios ....(ä′ dē ōs′)
Thank you .... gracias ....(grä′ sē äs)
God loves you ...... Dios te ama.......(dē ōs′ tā ä′ mä)

34

E A Mobile of Faithfulness.

Color the pictures on both sides of this page. Then cut out the hand and make a mobile.

A Bible Storybook.

מְנֵא מְנֵא
תְּקֵל
וּפַרְסִין

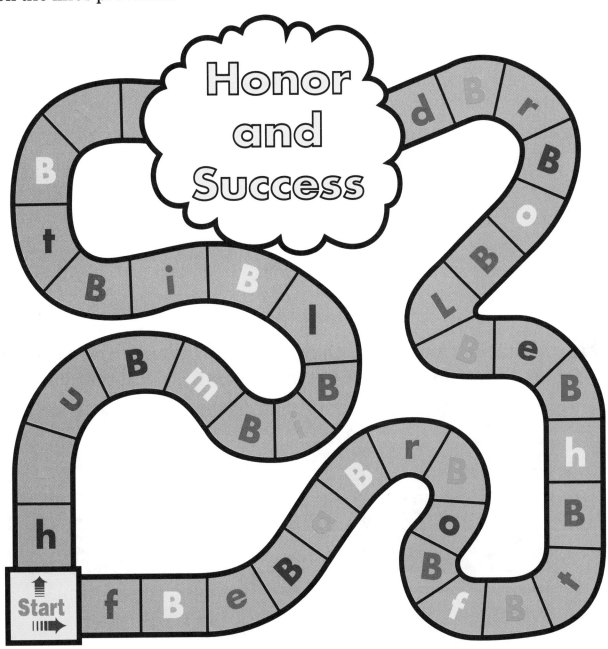

B **The Path to Honor.** Cross out every letter **B** on the puzzle below to find the two things God says will lead to honor and success. Look up Proverbs 22:4 in your Bible to see if you are correct. Write the answers on the lines provided.

Honor and Success

Start

_____ and

_____ bring honor.

C   **God's Protection.** As a wise man in Belshazzar's kingdom, Daniel fulfilled his responsibility to the king the night the writing appeared on the wall. Look at Daniel 5:26-28. What did the message say about Belshazzar's future as a king?

_____

_____

What can you learn from Daniel's example?

_____

_____

D   **A Timeline for Daniel.** Draw a line from the picture on the timeline to the character trait that best represents Daniel in that situation.

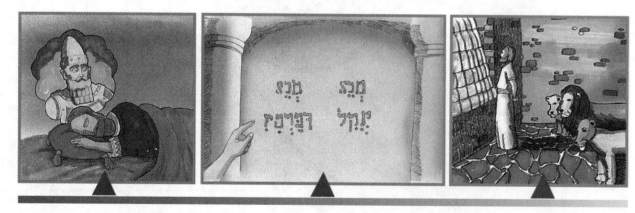

Confidence in God   Faithfulness   Humility   Courage   Obedience   Diligence

A **The Biggest "Little" Part of Me.** Look carefully at the three pictures below as your teacher talks about each one. Listen carefully to discover which part of each picture you are to circle.

B **Job's Words of Praise.** Read each statement that Job made. Look up each of the Bible references listed in the box below. Write the correct reference under each statement.

I know that my Redeemer lives.

I have kept His way and not turned aside.

References to find: Job 23:11, Job 19:25

C **Tiffany's Troublesome Tongue.**

D **Helping Words and Hurting Words.** As you look at each situation decide who is controlling the tongue well and who is not. Put a happy face by each good example and a sad face by each bad example.

E **Tongues of Praise.** It is good to give praise to God when things are going well and when they are not going well. Try singing the praise song below to the tune of "Mary Had a Little Lamb." This song will help remind you to praise God in all situations.

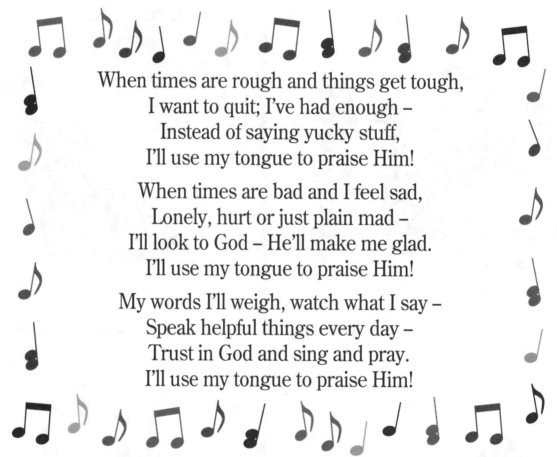

When times are rough and things get tough,
I want to quit; I've had enough –
Instead of saying yucky stuff,
I'll use my tongue to praise Him!

When times are bad and I feel sad,
Lonely, hurt or just plain mad –
I'll look to God – He'll make me glad.
I'll use my tongue to praise Him!

My words I'll weigh, watch what I say –
Speak helpful things every day –
Trust in God and sing and pray.
I'll use my tongue to praise Him!

F **Sweet Notes, Sour Notes.** Color each note for something you should remember.

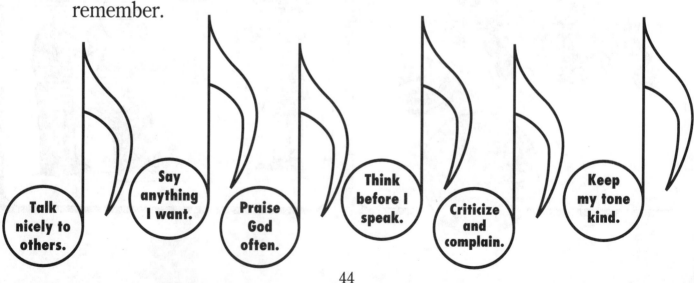

Talk nicely to others.

Say anything I want.

Praise God often.

Think before I speak.

Criticize and complain.

Keep my tone kind.

44

A **Patience at Work.** Look carefully at each picture below and read each verse. Draw a line from a verse to the situation which applies to it.

Romans 12:12

Ecclesiastes 7:8b

Proverbs 17:17

Proverbs 15:18

B **The Late Night Birthday Party.** Look at each picture as your teacher reads the story aloud. When the story is finished put a number by each picture to show the order in which it happened.

C  **When Bad Things Happen, What Can I Do?** Write a rhyme or words about having patience even when things are difficult. Sing it to a tune you know, or make up a tune or rhythm of your own. Color in the musical notes when you are finished.

When things go bad and I am sad,
I can be patient.

_____

_____

_____

D **Are You a Patient Patient?** Being patient can mean waiting for someone or something. Sometimes it means enduring or persevering. After learning about Job's patience this week, think about your own life. Circle the statement below which tells how patient you are. Patience is something God wants all Christians to have in their lives.

My patience is small.

My patience is growing.

My patience is big and getting bigger.

E **Amazing Job.** Help Job find his way through this maze to find the word **patience**.

F **What Does Patience Mean?** Find the word **patience** in your glossary and read the definition. Then write in your own words what **patience** means.

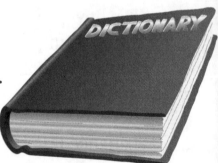

12

A **Preparing for a Queen.** Carefully color this picture of Queen Esther.

B **Advice for Life.** Today you have learned more about the benefits of listening to good advice. Find Proverbs 19:20 in your Bible and write it. Then write how you will obey this verse.

Proverbs 19:20

C **My Best Counselors.** Find Proverbs 1:8-9 to help you answer the question below.

1. Which two people give you counsel that you should listen to and follow?

_____ and _____

2. Circle the pictures of these two very beautiful things that people sometimes wear. The Bible says that when we listen to our parents and follow their instructions, our lives will be beautiful. Other people will notice that we have respect for our parents and will want to be our friends.

D **The Reward of Listening to Good Counsel.** Follow these directions for coloring the mosaic below. Color the **h**'s red, the **m**'s blue, and the **x**'s green. When you are finished, you will discover a word which describes a person who wants to follow God's counsel. Write the word on the blank line to complete the sentence at the bottom of the page.

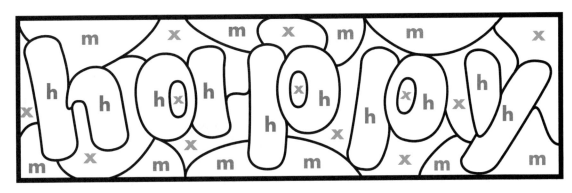

Blessed or _____ is the person who listens to God.
(Psalm 1:1)

51

E **Choosing Good Advice.** Read each situation below. Circle the advice which would help the person.

1. Kathy used to enjoy going to school every day. For the last month, two of the girls in her class have been laughing at her. She wants them to stop, but she isn't sure what to do.

Kathy could ignore them and just hope that they will stop teasing.

Kathy could talk to the girls about the problem. If they didn't stop, she could ask her parents for help.

2. Jonathan is eight years old. His best friend, Erik, moved to another state six days ago. Jonathan has missed his friend.

Jonathan could (without his parent's permission) call and talk with Erik for a little while.

Jonathan could pray and ask God to help him become friends with other boys at school or in his neighborhood.

 Order Restored. Listen to your teacher tell the story of Esther. Then number the pictures in the correct order.

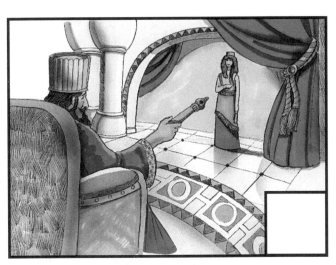

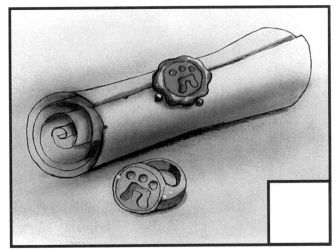

B **Selfish or Unselfish?** Search the picture below looking for unselfish actions. Circle all you find. Cross out all selfish actions you find.

C **Taking a Closer Look at Unselfishness.** Find and read the Bible verses. Draw a line from each Bible verse to the matching picture which shows unselfishness.

Genesis 45:21-23

John 3:16

Genesis 13:8-9

D **Dear Esther.** Write a letter to Esther telling her something in which you can be unselfish.

Dear Esther,

Sincerely,

A **Elijah Trusted God.** Cut out the ravens and follow your teacher's directions to make a mobile.

B **What God Provides.** Cut out each triangle and follow your teacher's directions.

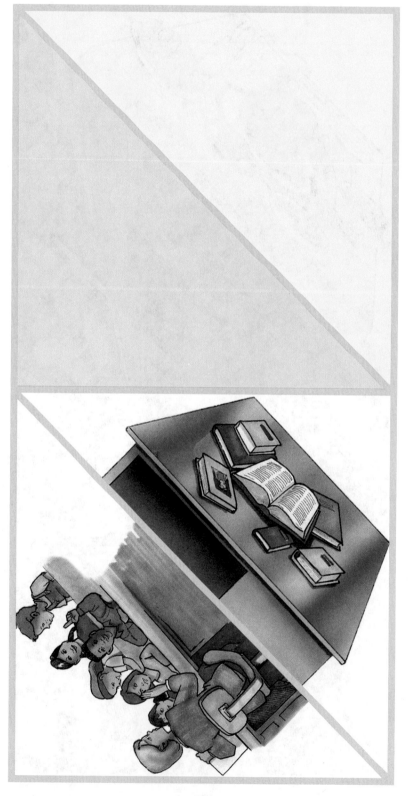

 A

The Mt. Carmel Gazette. Complete the newspaper article below by using the word bank to fill in information on the blank lines.

Mt. Carmel GAZETTE

Today's Words

Lord	nothing
water	minds
sent	Carmel
Ahab	fire
450	

Today's Weather
Drought Soon Over! Cooler with black clouds, strong winds and heavy rain.

Yesterday, something amazing happened on Mount _____.

Elijah told King _____ to invite the prophets of Baal and many Israelites to a big challenge.

Elijah told the Israelites to make up their _____. They needed to worship the Lord. The _____ prophets of Baal built an altar and prayed for their god to send _____. All day long _____ happened.

Then Elijah rebuilt the altar of the _____ and prayed one time to Him. The Lord _____ fire and burned up everything, including the _____!

The people bowed down and said, ...

Go to page 2.

B **The Rest of the Story.** To discover what the Israelites said, use a yellow crayon to color each shape with a dot. Color every other shape a different color.

C A Booklet of Colors.

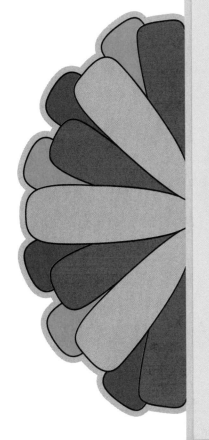

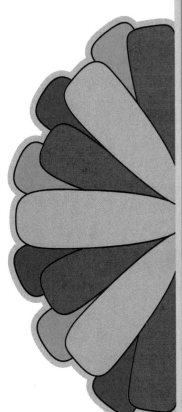

God loved
us and sent
His Son. *(John 3:16)*

Salvation is
God's free gift.
Pray and tell
God you want
to accept
His gift.
(Romans 6:23)

A **A Special Birth Announcement.** Use your Bible to complete the important information God announced about His Son.

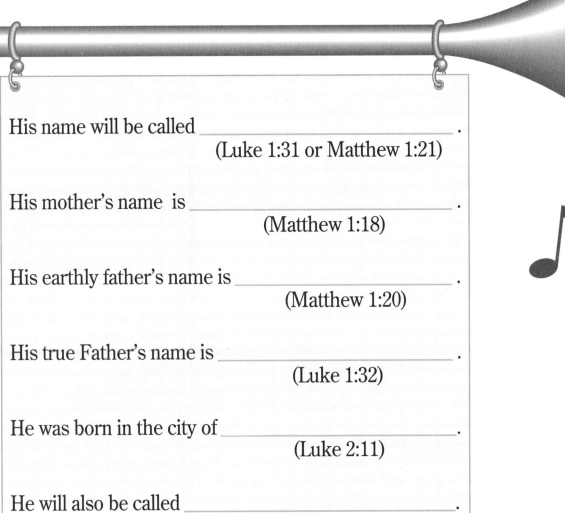

His name will be called _____ .
(Luke 1:31 or Matthew 1:21)

His mother's name is _____ .
(Matthew 1:18)

His earthly father's name is _____ .
(Matthew 1:20)

His true Father's name is _____ .
(Luke 1:32)

He was born in the city of _____ .
(Luke 2:11)

He will also be called _____ .
(Luke 1:35)

His _____ will never end.
(Luke 1:33)

B **Important Messages for God's People.** Tape each end of the angel's string to an **X**. Draw a line from each person to the correct message.

Luke 1:30

Matthew 1:20-21

Luke 2:10-11

"Don't be afraid to make Mary your wife ... ."

"Don't be afraid. I bring you good news ... ."

"Don't be afraid ... you have found favor with God."

C

Sending Out the Message of Christmas. Carefully cut out each picture and fold on the dotted line. Glue each set back to back.

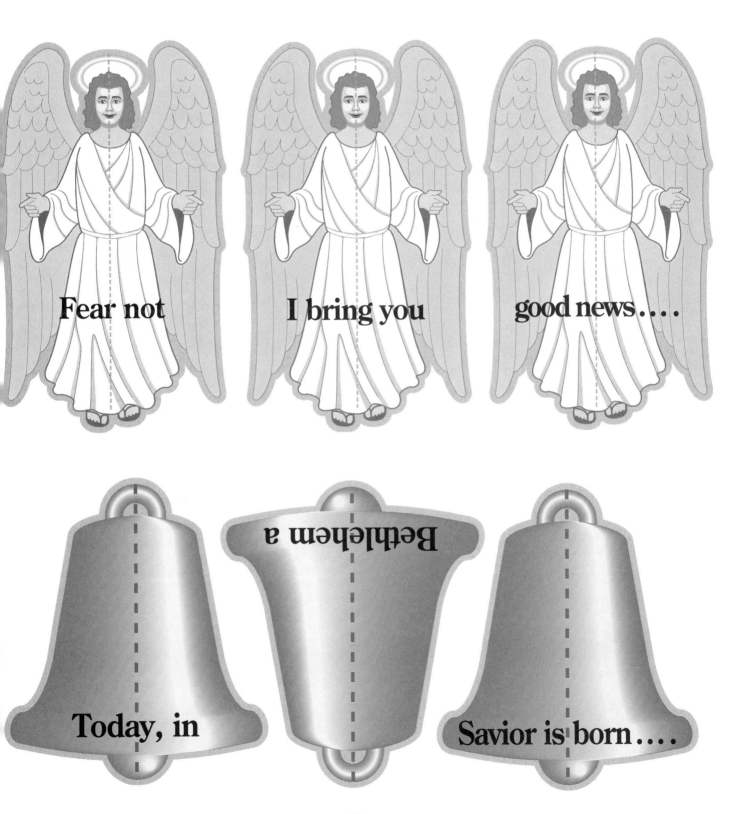

Fear not

I bring you

good news....

Today, in

Bethlehem a

Savior is born....

A   **Jesus Heals.** Write a title on the first page of your booklets. Complete the Bible verses on the back pages.

Jesus, _____ of

_____, have

_____ on me!

Luke 18:38

Luke 18:35-43

Son, _____ sins

are _____

_____ .

Mark 2:5

Mark 2:1-12

B **Mercy Maze.** Travel through the maze avoiding the two words not related to mercy. When you finish, color those words which help describe the word **merciful**.

C **Acrostic Response.** Using each word provided, write a phrase to describe merciful.

M ore _____

E ver _____

R eally _____

C areful to _____

I nstantly _____

F aithful to _____

U sually _____

L etting others _____

A

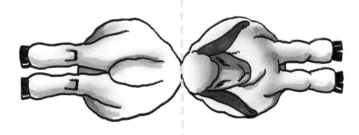

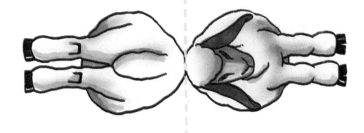

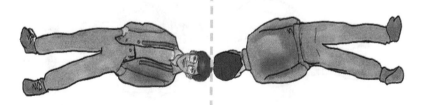

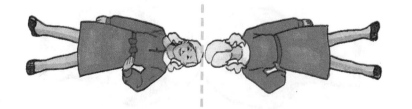

B Make a Booklet.

But when He saw
the multitudes,
He was moved
with compassion
for them, because
they were weary
and scattered,
like sheep having
no shepherd.

Matthew 9:36

A **Picture Parts.** Cut out each picture below and place it in the correct order from left to right in two columns. Tape the pictures together on each seam and turn the page over to reveal an important picture.

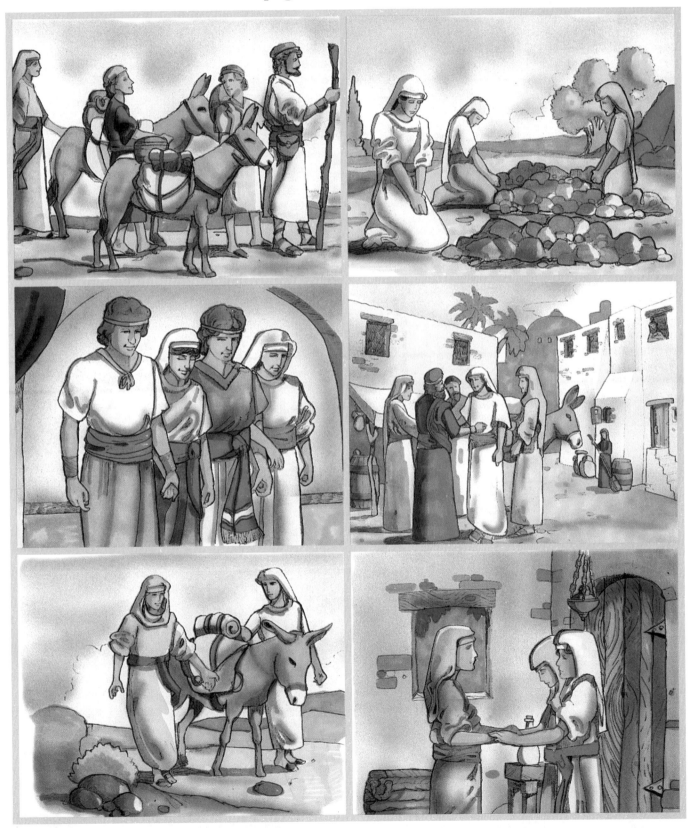

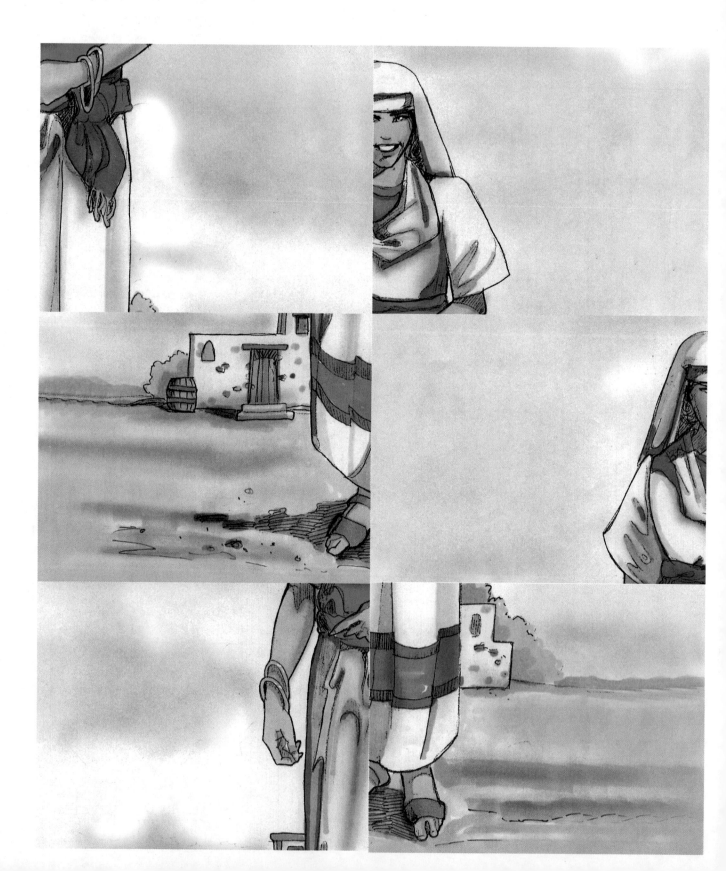

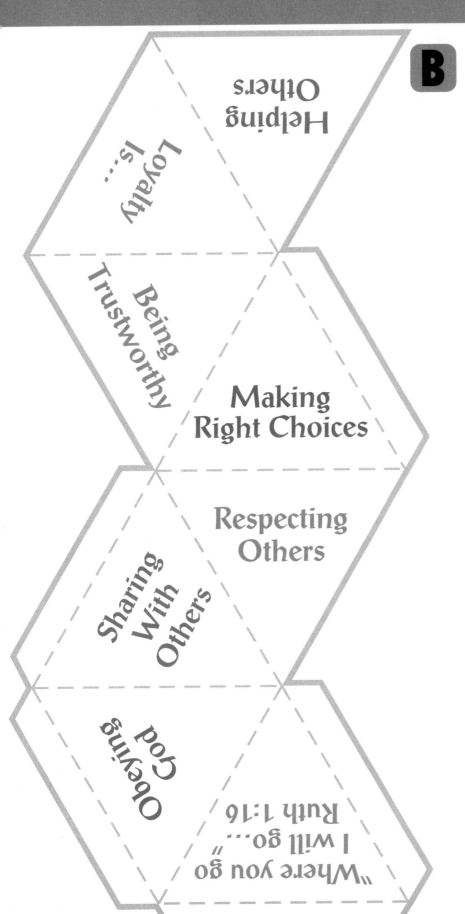

B **Loyalty Mobile.** Read each triangle and think of an example of how you can show loyalty. If you can think of a way to show loyalty for that item, color the triangle green. Then, cut out the mobile on the solid lines. Fold the mobile on the dotted lines. Glue or tape the tabs together and attach a string.

Helping Others

Loyalty Is...

Being Trustworthy

Making Right Choices

Respecting Others

Sharing With Others

Obeying God

"Where you go I will go..." Ruth 1:16

A **The Story of Ruth.** Remove this page from your book. Carefully cut out the four cards and Ruth's picture along the solid lines. Then gently fold each of the baskets of wheat across the center and with your scissors snip the solid line. This will create a slit on each basket. Arrange each of the cards in the correct story order.

B **A Gift of Character.** Look at the opposite side of the Exercise A pieces. On the bottom half of each character card write the name of a person for whom you could demonstrate these qualities. Then draw a picture of yourself behind the gifts.

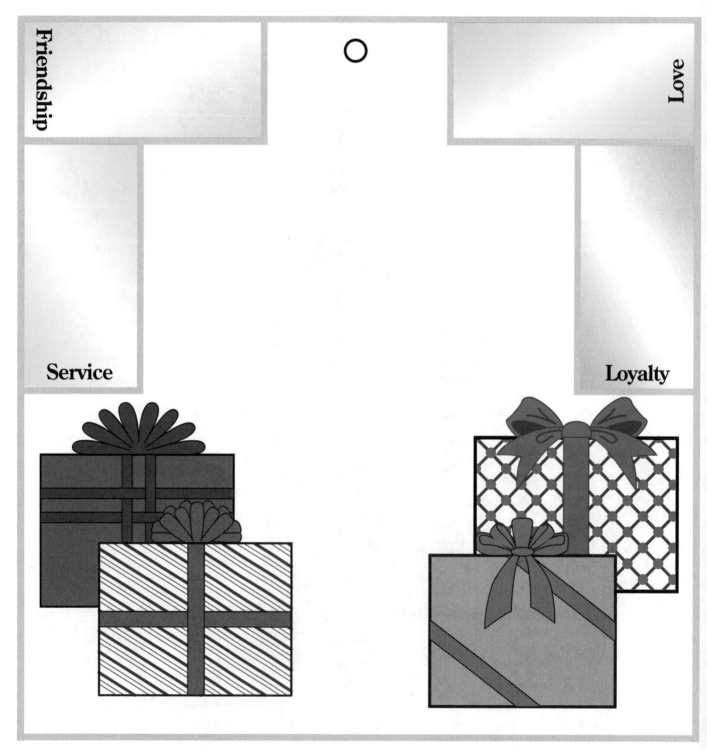

Friendship

Love

Service

Loyalty

C **In Love Serve.**   Follow your teacher's directions.

In Love Serve

D **Ruth and Naomi.** Match each sentence beginning with its correct ending.

1. Elimelech, Naomi and their sons	all died.
2. The sons grew up and	moved to Moab.
3. The wives were	named Orpah and Ruth.
4. The husbands of Naomi, Orpah and Ruth	married wives.
5. Ruth moved to Bethlehem	belonged to Boaz.
6. Ruth gleaned in fields that	with Naomi.
7. Boaz loved Ruth and	had a son named Obed.
8. Boaz and Ruth	married her.

 **A Fun Fact About Ruth.** Look carefully at the words written below. Can you figure out what it says? Below each letter is a blank box. Look at the first example done for you. Write the letter of the alphabet which comes after each letter you see.

Q T S G   V Z R   J H M F   C Z U H C ' R

[R] [U] [T] [H]   [ ] [ ] [ ]   [ ] [ ] [ ] [ ]   [ ] [ ] [ ] [ ] [ ]   [ ]

F Q D Z S   F Q Z M C L N S G D Q

[ ] [ ] [ ] [ ] [ ] - [ ] [ ] [ ] [ ] [ ] [ ] [ ] [ ] [ ] [ ] .

A **Story Viewer.** Cut each row on the lines going across. Put each row in the correct story order and tape the ends. Thread the first frame of the view strip into the right side of the envelope viewer and pull the strip through from right to left.

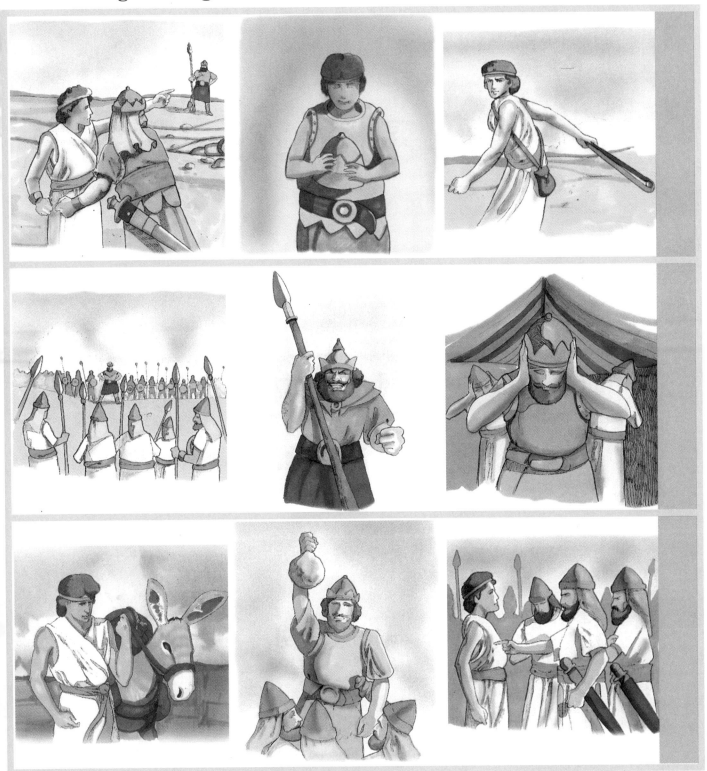

1 Samuel 17:47   is the Lord's!   for the battle

that the Lord   shall know   Then all this assembly

and spear;   with sword   does not save

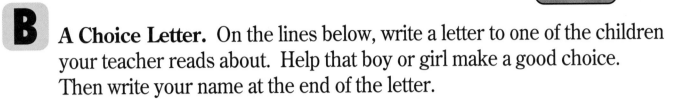

B **A Choice Letter.** On the lines below, write a letter to one of the children your teacher reads about. Help that boy or girl make a good choice. Then write your name at the end of the letter.

Dear _____,

_____

_____

_____

_____

_____

_____

_____

_____

_____

C **Crossword Puzzle Review.** Complete the crossword puzzle by reading the clues and using the word bank. Each word is used only one time.

Word Bank

battle
Goliath
David
Ruth
gleaning
Loyalty
widow
Love

1. The ___ is the Lord's. (1 Samuel 17:47)

2. Who was the young shepherd boy who fought Goliath?

3. What is another name for a woman whose husband has died?

4. Gathering bits of food left over from the harvest is called ___ .

5. Who was the champion fighter of the Philistine army?

6. ___ is sticking up for your friend no matter what.

7. ___ your neighbor as yourself. (Galatians 5:14)

8. Who became David's great-grandmother?

A **Travel Plans for Joab.** Write a number in the circle near the region to show the order in which Joab and his men arrived in ea Then draw a line between numbers 1-8 to show the travel route.

Mediterranean Sea

Sidon

Dan
Jaan

Tyre

Gilead

CANAAN

GAD

Jerusalem
1

Beersheba

B **Uncovering David's Sin.** Find the answers to the crossword puzzle clues and write them in the squares. Then copy the letters in the colored squares to uncover David's sin.

Word Bank

plague   called   sinned   altar   Beersheba

David's

displeased God.

1. Joab went from _____ to Dan counting the people. (1 Chronicles 21:2)
2. David realized he had _____. (1 Chronicles 21:8)
3. God sent a _____ because of David's sin. (1 Chronicles 21:14)
4. God told David to build an _____. (1 Chronicles 21:18)
5. David _____ on the Lord and the Lord answered him. (1 Chronicles 21:26)

Thumbs Up or Thumbs Down. Read the stories and circle the up or down thumb to show which kind of pride each child has.

1. Jordan likes to arm wrestle with the other boys in his class. He has won every contest so far this year. He brags about his ability nearly all the time.

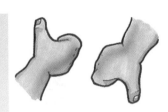

2. Marilyn loves to draw animal pictures. Several people have told her she draws very well. She knows she draws very well and never thanks people for their compliments. Once she entered a pet poster contest and won. She said, "I knew mine would be the best."

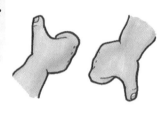

3. Michael and his brother, Tom, both competed in the second-grade spelling bee. They both qualified for the final round. Tom felt badly when he misspelled the word "numeral"; but he was very proud of his brother who spelled it correctly, then went on to win the competition.

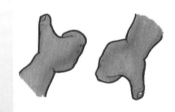

4. Lindsay and her family raise and show German shepherds. During her last dog show competition she received a first place ribbon. She was very happy to receive the reward, but she also gave much of the credit to her dog, Gandalph, for following directions so well.

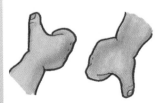

D Sin's Solution.

If we confess our sins,
He is faithful and just to
forgive us our sins…
1 John 1:9

Write in your own words
what David did to receive
forgiveness.

Write in your own words what
Christians do today to receive
forgiveness.

E

My Attitude. Think about what you have done today, or
another time, that was sinful. Talk to God about it and
then color the hands if you asked God to forgive you.

I have asked God to forgive my sin.

A Help Nehemiah find his way to Jerusalem.

B **Learning about Cooperation.** Color the areas with dots yellow to reveal the definition for cooperation. Color other shapes in the design in bright colors to create a mosaic.

C **Teamwork?** Circle every phrase which requires cooperation for success.

playing on a team

skating to win

watching T.V.

singing in chapel

cleaning the house

reading a book

making a bed

tying my shoes

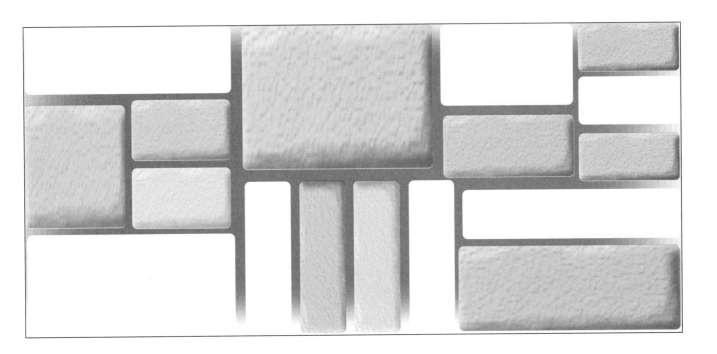

D **Helpful Actions for Rebuilding.** Cut out the stones below which describe cooperation and glue them into the correct shapes on the wall.

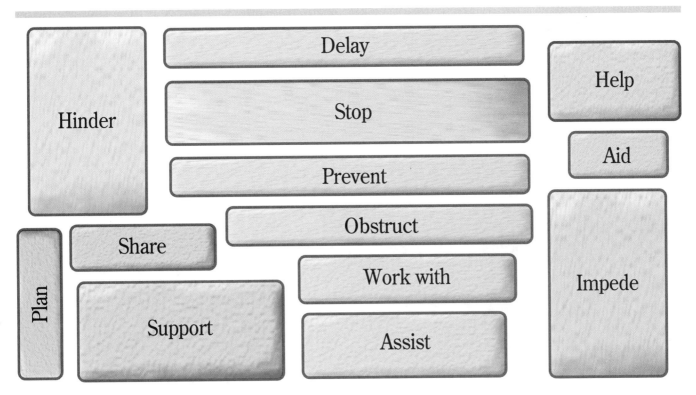

Delay

Stop

Prevent

Obstruct

Work with

Assist

Hinder

Share

Plan

Support

Help

Aid

Impede

E Who Is Cooperating? Place a circle around the pictures of cooperation and mark an **X** over two pictures that do not show cooperation.

A **Nehemiah Faces the Crowd.** Follow your teacher's directions.

We would like for you to come to our church.

We really have fun when we learn about Jesus.

Jesus loves you and wants to be your friend.

Jesus did die, but He's alive today. You can learn about that if you come Sunday.

C **My Prayer.** Read each line and write the phrase: Lord, help me stand.

When people tease me,

_____

When no one wants to be my friend,

_____

When I am pressured to do wrong things,

_____

When people say untrue things about me,

_____

D **Who Said It?** Write each statement under the person who said it. Use these Bible references to help you, if needed.

Nehemiah 4:4, 14; 6:9.   1 Chronicles 21:2, 8.

David 	Nehemiah 

I have sinned.

Hear, O our God!

Do not be afraid of them.

Go, number the Israelites.

O God, strengthen my hand.

Name

Hello there! Inspector Firestone's my name.
I'm searching for a responsible student.
Please identify yourself on the line below.

RESPONSIBILITY JOURNAL

This is to certify that

has been Responsible

Seal of Responsibility

_____
(signed)

_____
(date)

Inspector Firestone's Word Search

Can you help me find all the words that describe responsibilities by circling each one?

E	W	K	L	A	T	F	W	R
R	A	K	E	I	O	B	E	Y
L	S	A	H	K	L	E	H	G
I	H	Y	A	D	L	F	E	I
S	H	D	U	S	T	N	L	V
T	F	P	S	W	E	E	P	E
E	U	L	O	N	F	U	F	P
N	L	S	A	F	A	E	O	R
C	L	E	A	N	I	L	R	A
S	T	O	D	I	T	O	G	C
S	F	O	R	G	H	V	I	T
W	L	M	O	P	F	E	V	I
E	L	O	N	K	U	E	E	C
S	T	U	D	Y	L	K	F	E
D	I	P	R	A	Y	P	F	G
D	I	L	I	G	E	N	T	O

Word Bank

dust	sweep	help
clean	listen	love
study	obey	faithful
pray	mop	diligent
give	wash	practice
rake	forgive	

B Miriam Is Responsible for Moses

Mother: Miriam, do you understand what you are supposed to do?

Miriam: Yes, I will put the basket in the tall grass by the edge of the river and hide to watch it. But what do I watch for?

Father: We can't tell you exactly what will happen, but we believe God will do something wonderful. Your job is very important. If you don't stay to watch, we may never know what happens to your baby brother.

Mother: Don't be afraid. God will protect all of us.

Narrator: So Miriam took her place in the tall grass by the river. Maybe she had to squat down so no one would see her...and after a while, her legs began to feel very, very tired. The water probably got her dress wet, and the mud may have squished between her toes. Perhaps the flies and mosquitoes kept buzzing around her face and landing on her arms. She may have even heard the voices of her friends playing nearby. Oh, how she wanted to stretch her legs, put on a dry dress, and get away from those bugs! But she had been given a job to do and she was going to finish it. Then, a new sound filled the air...someone was coming to the river. Miriam peeked up above the grass. It was the princess, Pharaoh's daughter, and her maid! Was this the wonderful thing God was going to do?

Cut out puppets and tape around each finger.

Maid

Mother

Father

Miriam

Princess

Princess: Listen. What's that sound? Do you hear someone crying? Oh, look! There's a basket by the edge of the water. Hurry and bring it to me!

Maid: Look, Princess! It's a baby! What shall we do with him?

Princess: He is one of the Hebrew children! Poor thing! Let's take him back to the palace. I would love to have a son of my very own.

Narrator: Miriam jumped up from her hiding place. Her legs were tingling and the water splashed all over her as she hurried up to Pharaoh's daughter, but she didn't care.

Miriam: Princess, would you like me to find a mother to feed and care for your baby?

Princess: Yes, bring her to me. And when the baby is old enough, he will come to live with me in the palace as my son.

Narrator: Miriam rushed home to tell her parents what God had done. She was so glad she had stayed in the grass to watch. She didn't even remember how tired her legs were or how many flies had buzzed around her face! She had been a responsible girl — she followed her parents' instructions and finished her job. God had kept her baby brother safe, and she had been a part of it all!

A **Instruments for Praise.** Find the instruments listed below in the picture of praise. Circle each instrument.

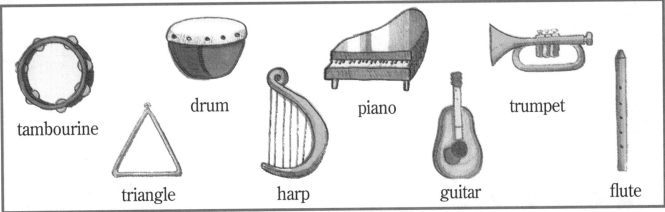

tambourine   drum   piano   trumpet

triangle   harp   guitar   flute

B **My Words of Praise.** Complete the sentence with some words of praise about God.

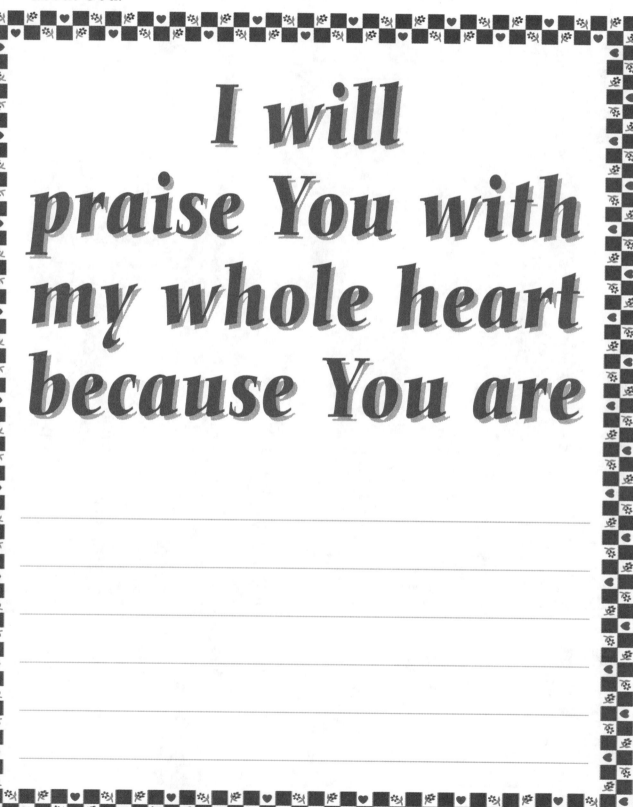

I will praise You with my whole heart because You are

_____

_____

_____

_____

_____

_____

C **Investigate a Hymn of Praise.** Look carefully at the hymn of praise. Use a blue crayon to underline words which praise God and a red crayon to underline words which tell about the wonderful things He has done.

Praise Him! Praise Him!
Fanny J. Crosby

1. Praise Him! Praise Him! Jesus, our blessed Redeemer!

   Sing, O Earth, His wonderful love proclaim!

   Hail Him! Hail Him! highest archangels in glory;

   Strength and honor give to His holy name!

   Like a shepherd, Jesus will guard His children,

   In His arms He carries them all day long:

2. Praise Him! Praise Him! Jesus, our blessed Redeemer!

   For our sins He suffered, and bled, and died;

   He our Rock, our hope of eternal salvation,

   Hail Him! Hail Him! Jesus the Crucified.

   Sound His praises! Jesus who bore our sorrows,

   Love unbounded, wonderful, deep and strong:

3. Praise Him! Praise Him! Jesus, our blessed Redeemer!

   Heavenly portals loud with hosannas ring!

   Jesus, Savior, reigneth forever and ever;

   Crown Him! Crown Him! Prophet and Priest and King!

   Christ is coming! Over the world victorious,

   Power and glory unto the Lord belong:

Chorus
Praise Him! Praise Him!
Tell of His excellent greatness:
Praise Him! Praise Him!
Ever in joyful song!

D **Who Should Praise the Lord?** Color in each area with a dot to find the hidden message.

A **Two Truths.** Follow each path to the Bible verse about respecting authority. Then complete the verses.

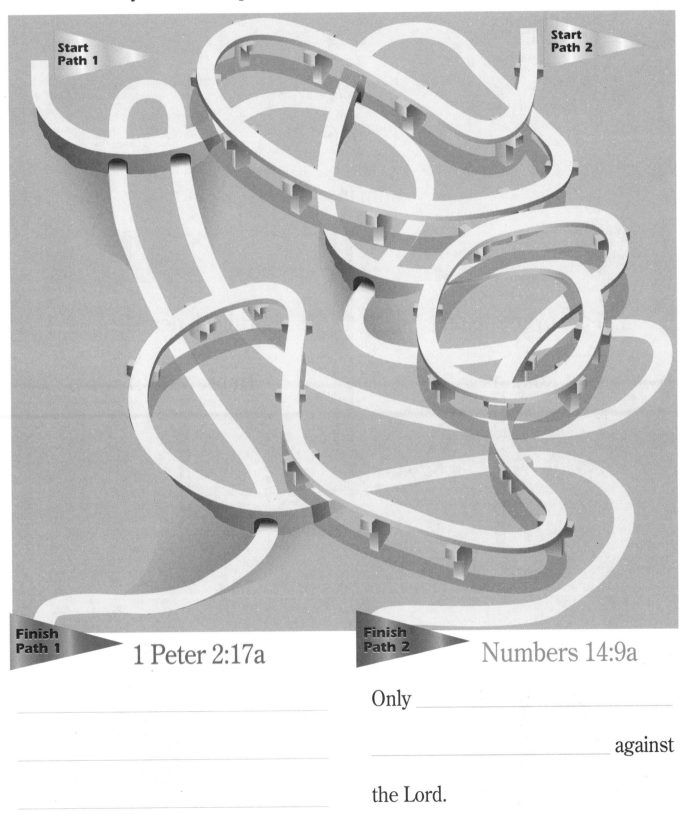

Finish Path 1   1 Peter 2:17a

Finish Path 2   Numbers 14:9a

Only _____

_____ against

_____   the Lord.

What the Bible Says about Authority. God uses authority to help and protect us. Read each Bible verse and unscramble the words which show your authorities.

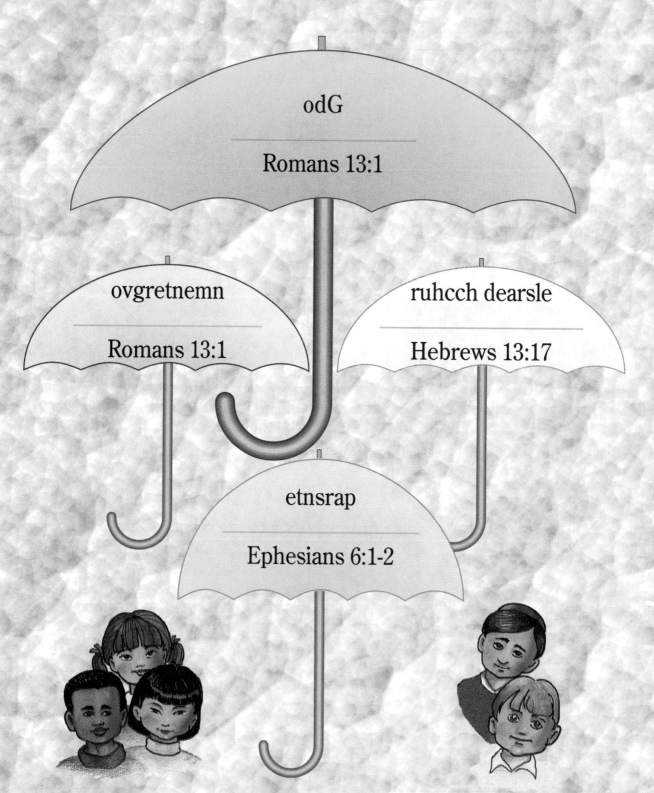

odG

_____

Romans 13:1

ovgretnemn

_____

Romans 13:1

ruhcch dearsle

_____

Hebrews 13:17

etnsrap

_____

Ephesians 6:1-2

C **Portraits of Authority.** Choose one of these people to write about on the lines below. Write at least one way you could show respect for this person's authority.

D **Detours to Disrespect.** Listen as your teacher reads a short story about each picture. Then draw a line to the reason for disrespect.

BECAUSE they destroyed someone's property.

BECAUSE he disobeyed the person in authority.

BECAUSE they did not remain quiet and listen as someone else was speaking.

BECAUSE he spoke badly and complained about another person.

BECAUSE he interrupted and talked back to someone.

BECAUSE they showed poor expressions with their faces and body.

A Cut out the booklet on the lines.

When Abraham was called to go
Into the Promised Land,
He listened and he followed —
And obeyed the Lord's command.

The wise man and the foolish man
Both listened to the Word.
The difference was that one obeyed
The things his ears had heard.

"Don't be just hearers," we are told,
"It's doers who are blessed."
Listening and obeying God
Will always be the best.

Staple completed pages here.

Carefully slit booklet
here to form a flap.

My Sheep Hear My Voice
(John 10: 4-5)

The sheep will hear their Shepherd,
And His voice they will obey —
Do what He says, go where He leads,
And trust Him all the way.

B **Listening to God's Son.** God sent His Son, Jesus, to teach us many things. After we study the things Jesus said, what does God want us to do? Find the answer in Mark 9:7 and write it below.

_____

_____

_____

_____

C **Looking in the Mirror.** Use a mirror to read the message. Underline the two words which tell you to do something.

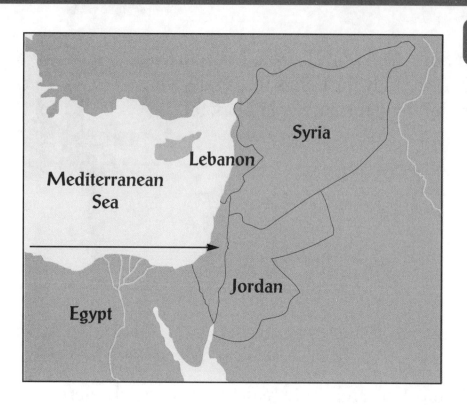

D **Abraham's Reward for Listening to God.** God used Abraham to begin a new nation of people. That nation uses the same name today. Read Exodus 3:14 to discover the name of this special nation and write it in the space provided on the map.

Read Matthew 1:1. Unscramble the names and discover two descendants of Abraham.

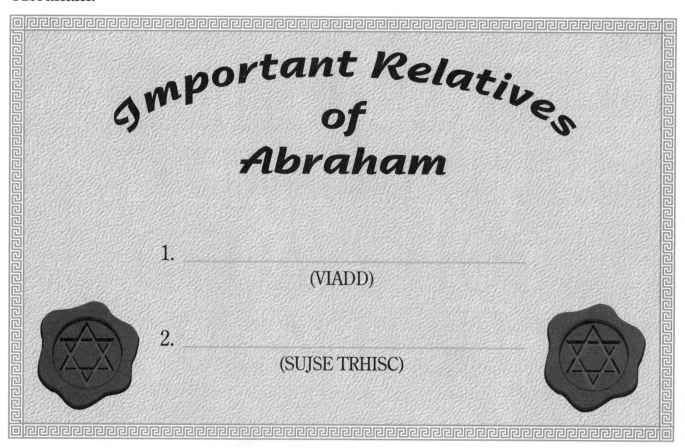

Important Relatives of Abraham

1. _____
   (VIADD)

2. _____
   (SUJSE TRHISC)

Abraham Learns Honesty

29

A **Abraham's Hard Lesson.** Cut apart the sentences and tape them in order to make a story.

Abraham was fearful of Pharoah and told Sarah to lie and say she was his sister.

Abraham learned an important lesson: God hates lies.

God was not pleased! He sent plagues and Pharoah knew something was wrong.

They decided to go to Egypt to find food.

When Pharoah learned Sarah was Abraham's wife, he sent them away.

Abraham and his family faced a great famine in Canaan.

Sure enough, Pharoah wanted to marry beautiful Sarah.

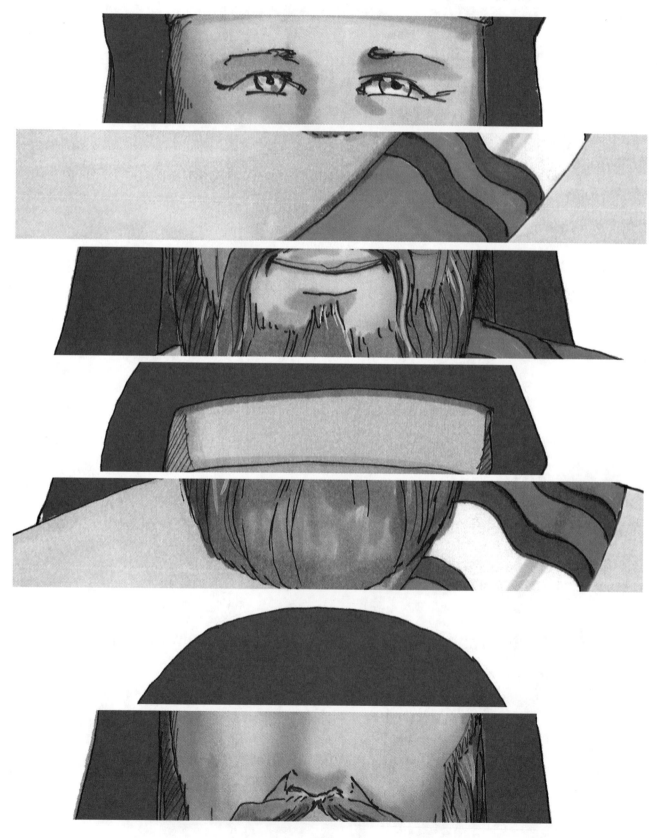

118

B The Whys of Lies.

THE WHYS OF LIES

If God hates a lie,
I wonder why I,
Who say that I love Him,
would let one get by?
It seems such a waste
to let my lips taste
The flavor of something
the God I love hates.

- fear of getting into trouble
- to get something that isn't mine
- wanting to get someone else into trouble
- to protect myself
- to make myself look good

> I think I left my watch here earlier. Have you seen it?

> No. I haven't seen any watches.

SCORE

| HOME | | | 2 | | | 1 | 3 | 0 | 0 | 0 | 6 |
| VISIT | | | | | | 1 | | | | | |

> I think I left my watch here earlier. Have you seen it?

Draw a picture of yourself under the blank speech balloon telling the boy the truth and returning the watch. Write the answer in the speech balloon above your head.

C The Lie Trap.

Please fold the clothes on the chair before I get home tonight.

Okay.

Tambi watched T.V.

Mom came home. Tambi stuffed the unfolded clothes into her closet when she heard the car.

Did you fold the clothes?

Yes, ma'am.

Tambi could have said…

Have you seen my blue socks?

No, ma'am.

Tambi could have said…

They were in those clothes you folded.

I didn't see them, Mom, honest.

Tambi could have said…

Oh, well. They'll turn up. I think this new top matches your red skirt. Let's look in your closet.

Tambi could have said…

A **Prayers Help Timmy.** Write the prayers of the people in the story your teacher reads. Then answer the questions below.

1. How did prayer help Timmy?

2. Why is it important to pray for others?

B **Jesus Prayed for Others.** Find John 17 in your Bible. Work with your teacher to fill in the blanks. Draw lines to match the verses with the correct sentences.

Jesus prayed for _____ (v. 9) and _____ (v. 20).
That includes _____.

Jesus prayed that believers would...

1. Have _____. (v. 13)

2. Be kept from _____.
   (v. 15)

3. Be _____.
   (v. 17)

4. Be _____. (v. 21)

5. Be with _____. (v. 24)

6. Have _____. (v. 26)

Be together, not separated by fussing and fighting.

Care for others and treat them with kindness.

Be happy, not sad.

Be saved and live with God forever.

Be protected, not hurt or harmed.

Be clean from sin and ready to serve.

122

C **Prayer Packets.** Cut out and assemble your prayer packet. Don't forget to pray for others!

Punch hole here.

Fold inward on all broken lines.

Punch hole and insert brass fastener. Cover it with tape.

My Prayer Packet

_____

Pray for one
another...
(James 5:16)

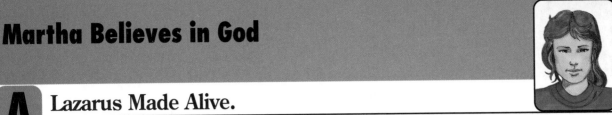
A **Lazarus Made Alive.**

Friends Need Help.

Martha, Mary and their brother Lazarus were Jesus' friends.

How can we let Jesus know that Lazarus is sick?

We can send Him a message saying, "Lord, the one You love is sick."

More Than a Friend.

Jesus and the disciples arrived in Bethany four days after Lazarus had been buried.

Lord, if You had been here, my brother would not have died.

I am the resurrection and the life. Martha, do you believe this?

How did Martha answer?

_____

_____

_____

John 11:27

"I am the resurrection and the life."
John 11:25

Lazarus Lives Again. After Martha told Mary that Jesus wanted to talk with her, they both showed Him Lazarus' tomb.

Take away the stone… Father, I thank You that You have heard Me… Lazarus, come _____!

C **What Jesus Said about Himself.** Read each clue for the crossword puzzle below. Write the correct word in each space. Use your Bible to help you. Then unscramble the four letters in the yellow squares to complete the verse below.

Down

1. Jesus said, "I am the _____ and the life." (John 11:25)

Across

1. Jesus said He came to seek and to _____ the lost. (Luke 19:10)

2. Jesus said those who had seen Him had seen the _____. (John 14:9)

3. Jesus said He had come as a _____ into the world. (John 12:46)

I have come that they may have _____. (John 10:10b)

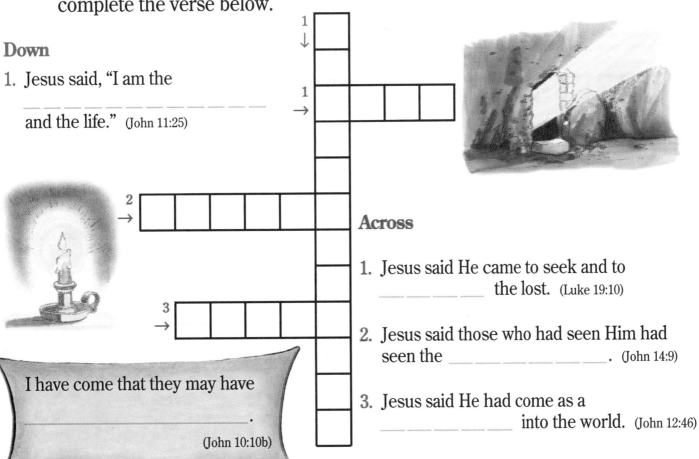

127

Many Believed. Many Jews followed Mary to the tomb and saw what Jesus did. Many believed, but some did not believe. Draw yourself in the crowd and write your answer to Jesus' question in your balloon.

Do you believe?

Yes.

I believe.

Yes.

Not me.

D **I Believe.** Look up the references that Mr. Johnson read to Timmy and Tina. Choose the one that you like the best and tell what it means on the lines below.

I Believe...

Signed: _____

Date: _____

A **Jill's Birthday Party.** Find and circle the wrong things happening at this party.

Write a letter explaining how the children should have shown self-control.

B The In's and Out's of Peter.

John 18:10-11

Acts 12:1-11

Luke 22:54-62

Acts 4:1-12

| He preached about Jesus. | He tried to solve the problem his own way. | He waited for God's help. | He denied knowing Jesus. |

C **Discovering the Source of Peter's Control.** Discover Peter's source of control by writing the first letter of each picture on the blank above it.

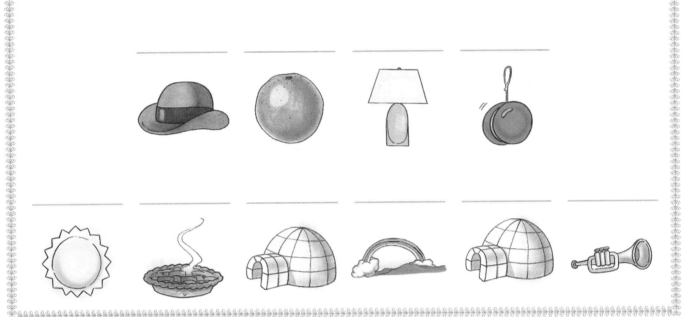

D **Another Name.** Color only the spaces with a dot. Write the word you discover on the line to complete the statement.

The Holy Spirit is my _____.

131

Holy Spirit, Be My Helper. Underline the words **Holy Spirit, be my Helper** with a red crayon when your teacher tells you to do so.

When I know I shouldn't giggle,
But my insides start to jiggle,
And my lips begin to wiggle —
Holy Spirit, be my Helper.

When I have to wait in line,
Way in back and far behind
And I want to start to whine —
Holy Spirit, be my Helper.

When I have to make my bed,
'Cause that's what my Mom has said,
And I want to play instead —
Holy Spirit, be my Helper.

Write what you asked the Holy Spirit to help you with.

_____

_____

_____

A **Peter's Lesson.** Write the numerals 1 to 6 in the boxes to show the correct order of each picture.

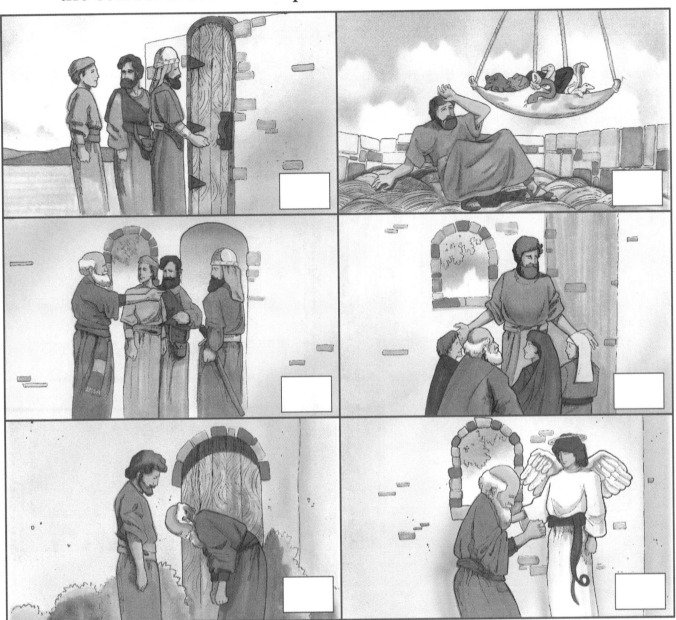

Read Acts 10:34-35

Write in your own words what Peter learned after preaching in Cornelius' home.

_____

_____

B **Partner Interviews.** Complete the information chart about yourself and about your partner.

God Made Me

Name_____

Birthday_____

Eye Color_____

Height_____

Brothers_____

Sisters_____

Draw a picture of something you like to do.

God Made You

Name_____

Birthday_____

Eye Color_____

Height_____

Brothers_____

Sisters_____

Draw a picture of something your partner likes to do.

We are alike because_____

We are different because_____

C Make a "Thumbody" Booklet. ✓

We're Thumbodies

I am fearfully and wonderfully made. *(Psalm 139:14b)*

A **Meet the Encouragers.** Use your Bible to complete the names of two Bible characters.

ACTS 4:36   ACTS 13:9

B_____   S_____

Son of   also called

_____   _____

B **Who's Encouraging Whom?** Read Acts 9:27 and write what is happening in this picture.

C

Encouragement Is.... Write the meaning of encouragement in your own words.

Encouragement is _____

_____

_____

_____

_____

D

Encouragement at Work. Match each situation on the left with the correct act of encouragement on the right.

1. Saul was a Christian. He needed to grow, but the believers in Jerusalem were afraid of him. What did Barnabas do to encourage him?

☐ They took offerings to them.

2. Saul spent three years in the desert studying about the Lord. Then he went back home. What did Barnabas do to encourage him?

☐ He took Saul to the disciples and introduced him.

3. The believers in Jerusalem were hungry because of a famine. What did Barnabas and Saul do to encourage them?

☐ He took Saul to Antioch and together they worked in the church.

E **Encourage One Another.** Use your Bible to fill in the blanks based on 1 Thessalonians 5:12-14. Then look for the words in the Word Search.

_____ those who _____ among you and are over you in the _____ (v. 12). Warn those who are _____ (v. 14), _____ the _____ (v. 14), _____ the weak (v. 14), be patient with _____ (v. 14).

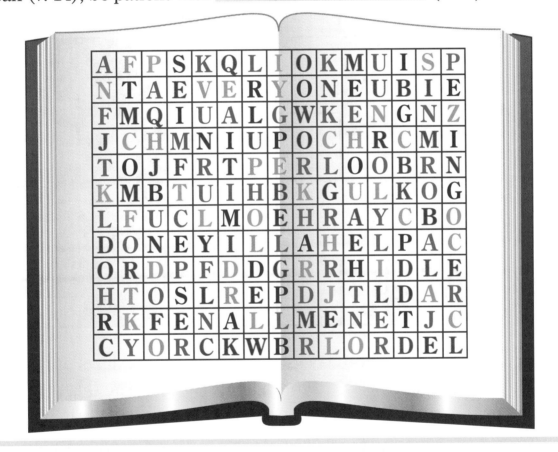

```
A F P S K Q L I O K M U I S P
N T A E V E R Y O N E U B I E
F M Q I U A L G W K E N G N Z
J C H M N I U P O C H R C M I
T O J F R T P E R L O O B R N
K M B T U I H B K G U L K O G
L F U C L M O E H R A Y C B O
D O N E Y I L L A H E L P A C
O R D P F D G R R H I D L E
H T O S L R E P D J T L D A R
R K F E N A L L M E N E T J C
C Y O R C K W B R L O R D E L
```

F **Encouragement Encounters.** Draw a happy face in the blank box in the picture if someone is giving and receiving encouragement. Draw a sad face in the box if there is no encouragement.

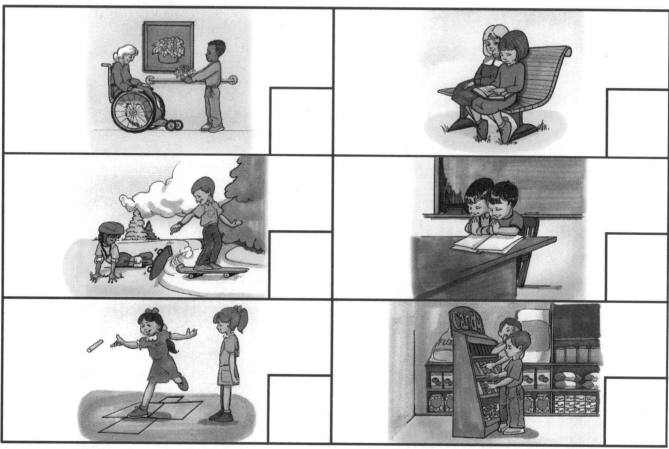

G **Barnabas Note.** Write 1 Thessalonians 5:11 on the lines provided. Cut this note on the line. Decide whom to give it to. Write that person's name on the front. Write an encouraging message on the other side.

Therefore _____

_____

and _____

_____

1 Thessalonians 5:11

TO:

A **Paul Shares with His Jailer.** Use one of your puppets as you read this play with a partner.

Narrator: Paul and his helper, Silas, were sitting in a jail cell in the city of Philippi. They were put there because they preached the Gospel and made some businessmen in the city angry. Their feet were locked in stocks to make sure they could not escape. Most people would be sad and discouraged, but they were not. They prayed and sang to God. Then, some wonderful things happened.

Paul: *(in a singing voice)* God is so very good and wonderful. I praise Him for…

Narrator: Suddenly, and without warning, the entire jail began to shake. The stocks popped open, the chains fell off the other prisoners, and even the doors on the cells popped open.

Paul: What an earthquake! Look! The stocks are open and all the prisoners are free!

Jailer: *(awakens and fears the worst)* What was all that noise and shaking? I better hurry downstairs and see what has happened! (pause) Oh, no! The cell doors are open. Someone, bring me a lamp! If any of the prisoners has escaped, the judge will have me killed!

Paul: *(shouting to the jailer)* Sir, we are all here! Don't harm yourself!

Jailer: No one has escaped? I can hardly believe you didn't run away! What must I do to be saved? Please tell me!

Paul: You must believe on the Lord Jesus Christ. Only He can save you.

Jailer: I believe! I do believe in Him!

Narrator: After the jailer believed in Jesus, he invited Paul and Silas to his home. He fed them and cleaned their wounds. The jailer's family also believed, and everyone was filled with joy.

B **Paul and Silas Witness.** Discover the ways Paul and Silas witnessed to others while they were in jail. Begin with the first letter at the left of each picture and circle every other letter. Write them in order on the lines below the picture. Then write the uncircled letters in order.

TEHDETYOPGROADY

TYHMENYSSTAONGGOHD

TTHREUYNDAIWDANYO

TLHEERYATBOOLUDTTJHEESJUASI

C **The Salvation Hand.** Write each verse reference from the Verse Bank in the correct box.

God loves me.

I am a sinner.

Jesus died for me.

I receive Him.

I have eternal life.

VERSE BANK

1 John 5:12

Romans 5:8

John 3:16

Romans 3:23

John 1:12

D Good-bye from Guatemala.

Timmy: It seems like we just introduced ourselves a little while ago.

Tina: We hope you enjoyed learning about some of the things that missionary families do in a far away place. Thank you for coming along.

Mrs. Johnson: Remember, missionaries are grateful for your prayers and help. Please remember to pray for them and help them by getting involved in the missions program at your church.

Mr. Johnson: We became missionaries to Central America because of the Great Commission. Jesus wants us to tell everyone about Him. Every Christian has a responsibility to tell others about Jesus. Think about someone you know who needs to hear the Good News. Write that person's name on the line below and tell how you can share the Good News with him or her.

All: ¡Adios, amigos!

Martha

A **Who Am I?** Draw a line from the Bible character to the correct statement.

Esther

I showed mercy when I healed the paralyzed man and the blind man.

I saw a burning bush and humbled myself before God.

I boldly challenged the 450 prophets of Baal on Mt. Carmel.

I was thrown into the lions' den for being faithful to God.

Elijah

Moses

I listened to the wise counsel of my uncle and became queen.

I obeyed God as I led the people in a march around Jericho.

I trusted God even when I lost everything.

I declared Jesus was the Son of God, and He could raise my dead brother, Lazarus.

Daniel

Joshua

Jesus

Job

B Remember Me? Draw a line from the Bible character to the correct statement.

Nehemiah

Silas

I was loyal to God and Naomi.

I witnessed to the jailer about Jesus.

I knew I could defeat Goliath because the battle belonged to the Lord.

Ruth

I learned to accept all people just as God does.

Miriam

I led the people to cooperate and stand against the crowd so the wall of Jerusalem could be rebuilt.

I led the women to praise God in the desert.

David

I listened to God and moved my family to Canaan.

I encouraged the disciples to accept Saul.

Barnabas

I helped Paul and was in jail with him.

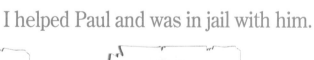

Peter

Paul

Abraham

C **My Favorite Character.** Write the name of your favorite Bible person on the line below and answer the questions. Then draw a picture of that person.

Name: _____

Why is this your favorite Bible person?

_____

_____

_____

_____

What is the most important thing you learned from this person's life?

_____

_____

_____

_____

D **My Commitment.** Think about all the things you have learned from God's Word this year. Choose two things you will do with God's help and write them below.

With God's Help...

I will _____

_____

_____

_____

_____

I will _____

_____

_____

_____

_____

Signature: _____

Date: _____

Glossary

Maps

◆ Glossary ◆

Aa

Abraham - 1. listened to God and moved with his family to Canaan 2. learned that God values honesty and wants His people to tell the truth 3. prayed for other people whom He did not know

accepting others - knowing that God loves all people even those different from me

Bb

Barnabas - 1. his real name was Joses 2. received the nickname, Barnabas, from other believers because he always encouraged people in many ways 3. helped and encouraged Paul

believing in God - asking God to save me and trusting Him to give me eternal life

bold - 1. being brave or courageous in difficult or even dangerous situations 2. choosing to do the right thing no matter what others are choosing to do

Cc

census - a count of the number of people in a particular area

compassionate - concern for the needs of others

confess - to admit to God or others that I have done something that is wrong

confident - believing or trusting in God because I do not doubt His ability to help me

control(led) tongue - saying good and helpful words and speaking praises to God

cooperate - working together to get a job done

counsel - information or advice given to help make a wise decision

courageous - 1. facing hard things bravely knowing God will help me 2. doing the right thing even when I am afraid

covenant - a promise never broken between people or between people and God, usually written down and signed

Dd

Daniel - 1. was taken from his homeland and forced to live in Babylon 2. was faithful to God in every situation 3. was chosen by three different kings to help govern Babylon 4. had a good mind and very healthy body

David - 1. as a young boy tended sheep for his father, Jesse 2. killed a lion and a bear with his hands 3. volunteered to fight the Philistine champion, Goliath 4. defeated Goliath with one shot from his sling and God's help

diligent - working hard to finish a task, never giving up

drought - a long time period when no rain falls, lakes and streams begin to dry up

Ee

Elijah - 1. a prophet of God 2. challenged the prophets of Baal on Mt. Carmel 3. depended on God during a drought 4. was bold for God

encourage - to share kind and gentle words with people and help them make right choices

Esther

Esther - 1. Queen of Persia selected by King Xerxes 2. raised by Mordecai 3. her name means star 4. risked her life to save her people 5. was very wise

Ff

faithful - following God even when it is difficult

famine - a long period of time when food is difficult or impossible to find, usually caused by a drought

following God wholeheartedly - 1. working for God with all my energy without complaining 2. worshipping God and no one else

Gg

Gentile - all people in the world who are not Jews

gleaning - gathering the produce left after a harvest has been completed

Hh

honesty - acting and speaking truthfully in all situations

humble - 1. not bold or proud 2. meek 3. to know our weaknesses and depend on God for strength

Jj

Jesus - 1. God's one and only Son 2. His birth was foretold by God's prophets and announced by God's angels 3. has the authority to heal and forgive sins 4. His name means the (Lord) One who saves 5. born in Bethlehem

Jew - a person who is a descendent of Abraham, Isaac and Jacob

Job - a righteous man who lived in a faraway land and worshiped God during good and bad times

Joshua - 1. Moses' special helper during the time of wandering in the desert 2. chosen by God to lead the Israelites into the promised land of Canaan after Moses died 3. led the Israelites at the Battle of Jericho

Ll

listening to God - reading the Bible to learn what God wants me to do and then doing it

loving God's Word - reading the Bible regularly and obeying God's instructions to me

loving servant - someone who cares for the needs of others with a good attitude

loyalty - being faithful to someone I care about no matter what

Mm

Martha - Jesus' friend and believed He was the Son of God

merciful - forgiving and treating people in a kind and caring way even when they don't deserve it

Miriam - 1. Moses' sister 2. helped Moses and Aaron lead the Israelites 3. On one occasion she did not give respect to Moses and suffered the consequences of her sin. She was healed after Moses prayed that she be forgiven.

Moses - 1. a humble leader of the Israelites 2. His name means drawn out.

Nn

Nehemiah - 1. served as the king's cupbearer 2. the governor of Jerusalem for twelve years 3. directed the rebuilding of Jerusalem in fifty-two days

Oo

obedience - 1. quickly doing what I am told with the right attitude 2. listening to and following directions

Pp

patience - waiting or enduring difficult times without complaining

Paul - 1. originally named Saul 2. became a Christian when Jesus spoke to him while traveling to Damascus 3. became an Apostle of Jesus Christ and led three important missionary journeys

Peter - 1. a fisherman and the brother of Andrew 2. called by Jesus to be His disciple 3. denied Jesus three times after saying he would never do such a thing 4. filled with the Holy Spirit at Pentecost 5. preached to others about Jesus

plague - a disaster or severe illness that effects large numbers of people and or animals, and can result in many deaths

praising God - telling God He is wonderful and that I love Him

prayer - talking with God

pride - 1. having a very high opinion of someone or something 2. can be a sin when it gets in the way of our relationship with God or other people

prophet - a person who announced God's words to people

Rr

repentance - being sorry for sin, confessing the sin and changing my actions

respect authority - obeying or following the directions of someone who is in charge over me without grumbling or complaining

responsible - 1. careful to follow directions and finish a task 2. being dependable and reliable

Ruth - 1. originally from Moab 2. married one of Naomi's two sons 3. became a widow 4. loyal to Naomi 5. King David's great grandmother

Ss

self-control - choosing to do right, even when I am tempted to do wrong

Silas - 1. a missionary who traveled with Paul 2. spent time in the Philippian jail with Paul

sin - 1. any action that is displeasing to God 2. the result of Adam and Eve's decision to disobey God

sorry for my sin - feeling badly that I have displeased God, confessing the action and making up my mind not to repeat it.

standing against the crowd - not giving in to pressures from others to do wrong.

successful - 1. having a good feeling or receiving a reward for doing my best 2. doing my best and finishing my task

Tt

temptation - something a person may want to do even though he or she knows it is wrong

threshing floor - a flat, open space on or near the top of a hill where grain was separated from the stalk

trusting in God - depending on God for His care for me

Uu

unselfish - placing the needs of others first

Ww

wise advice - information or counsel given to help make a wise decision

wise choices - using God's Word and listening to godly people to help me make good decisions

witnessing - telling others that Jesus died for their sins and if they believe in Him they can have eternal life

wholeheartedly - doing something with complete and sincere enthusiasm

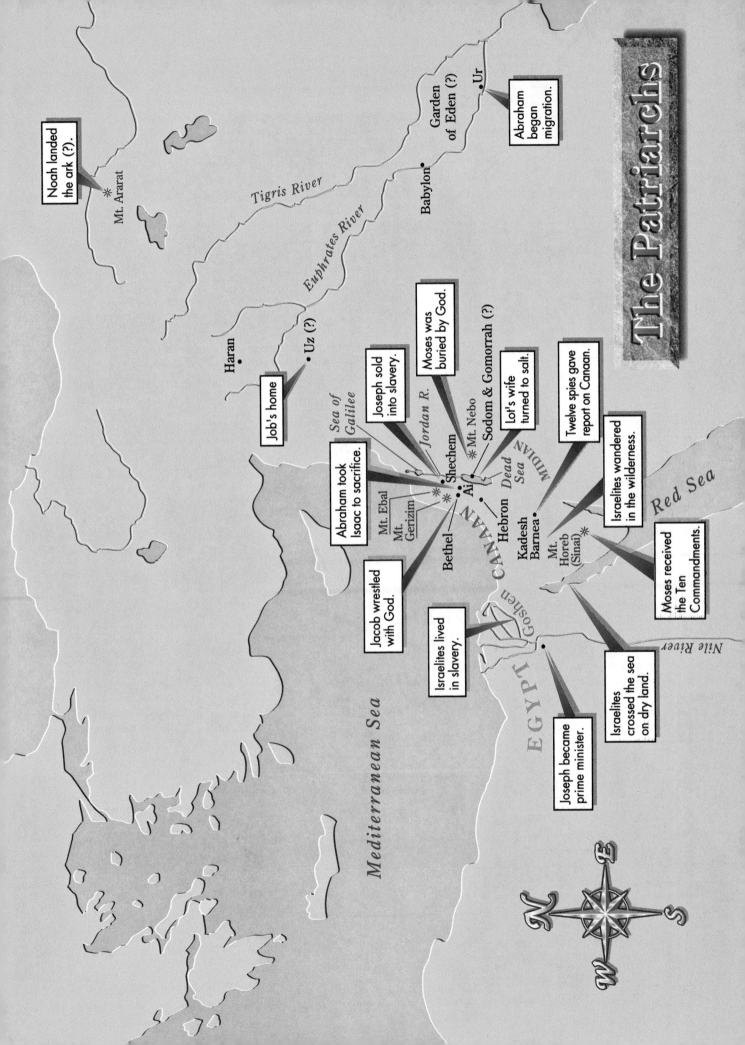

The Patriarchs

Noah landed the ark (?).

Mt. Ararat

Tigris River

Euphrates River

Garden of Eden (?)

Babylon

Ur

Abraham began migration.

Haran

Uz (?)

Job's home

Sea of Galilee

Joseph sold into slavery.

Moses was buried by God.

Jordan R.

Mt. Nebo

Sodom & Gomorrah (?)

Lot's wife turned to salt.

Dead Sea

Twelve spies gave report on Canaan.

Abraham took Isaac to sacrifice.

Shechem

Ai

MIDIAN

Mt. Ebal

Mt. Gerizim

Bethel

CANAAN

Hebron

Kadesh Barnea

Mt. Horeb (Sinai)

Israelites wandered in the wilderness.

Red Sea

Moses received the Ten Commandments.

Jacob wrestled with God.

Israelites lived in slavery.

Goshen

EGYPT

Nile River

Israelites crossed the sea on dry land.

Joseph became prime minister.

Mediterranean Sea

N E W S

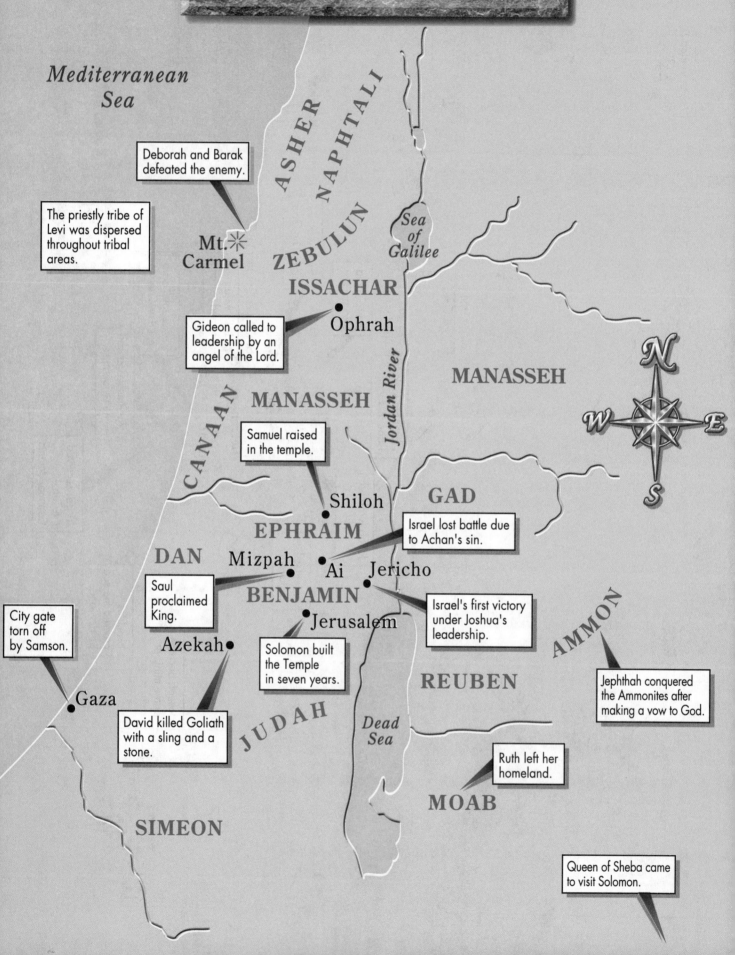

The Judges—United Kingdom

Mediterranean Sea

Deborah and Barak defeated the enemy.

The priestly tribe of Levi was dispersed throughout tribal areas.

ASHER

NAPHTALI

Sea of Galilee

Mt. Carmel

ZEBULUN

ISSACHAR

Gideon called to leadership by an angel of the Lord.

Ophrah

MANASSEH

Jordan River

MANASSEH

CANAAN

Samuel raised in the temple.

Shiloh

GAD

EPHRAIM

Israel lost battle due to Achan's sin.

DAN

Mizpah

Ai

Jericho

Saul proclaimed King.

BENJAMIN

Israel's first victory under Joshua's leadership.

City gate torn off by Samson.

Azekah

Jerusalem

Solomon built the Temple in seven years.

AMMON

Jephthah conquered the Ammonites after making a vow to God.

REUBEN

Gaza

David killed Goliath with a sling and a stone.

JUDAH

Dead Sea

Ruth left her homeland.

MOAB

SIMEON

Queen of Sheba came to visit Solomon.

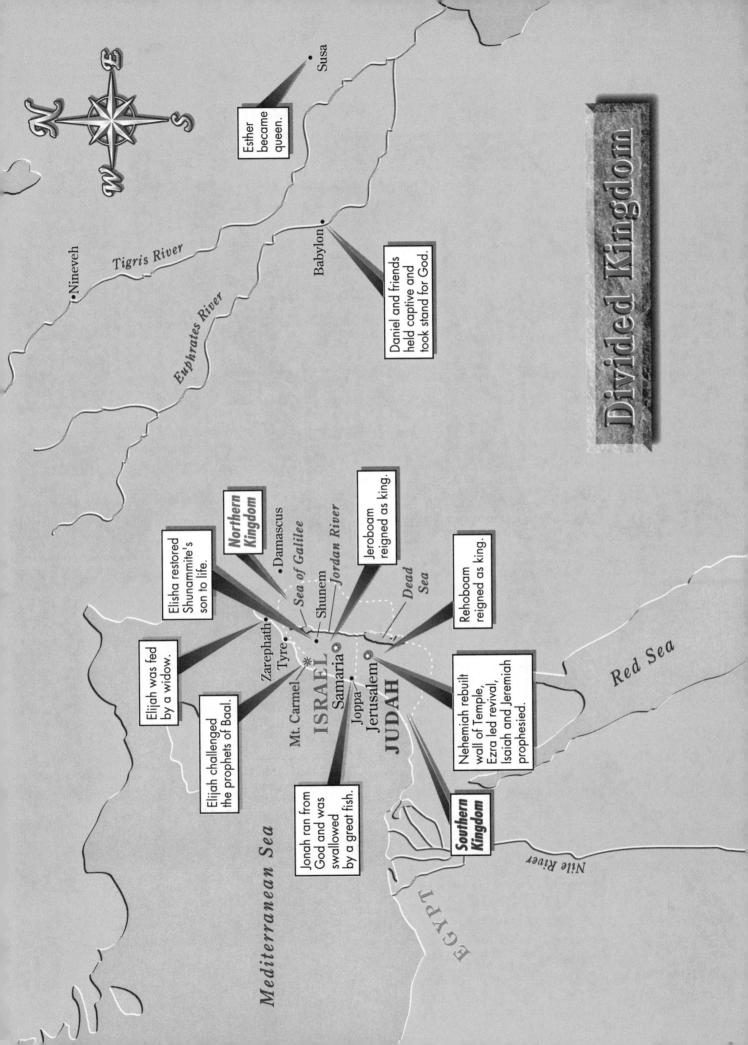

Divided Kingdom

Esther became queen.

Susa

•Nineveh

Tigris River

Euphrates River

Babylon

Daniel and friends held captive and took stand for God.

Northern Kingdom

•Damascus

Sea of Galilee

Shunem

Jordan River

Elisha restored Shunammite's son to life.

Jeroboam reigned as king.

Dead Sea

Rehoboam reigned as king.

Zarephath•

Tyre

Elijah was fed by a widow.

Mt. Carmel

ISRAEL

Samaria

Joppa

Jerusalem

JUDAH

Elijah challenged the prophets of Baal.

Nehemiah rebuilt wall of Temple, Ezra led revival, Isaiah and Jeremiah prophesied.

Red Sea

Jonah ran from God and was swallowed by a great fish.

Southern Kingdom

Mediterranean Sea

Nile River

EGYPT

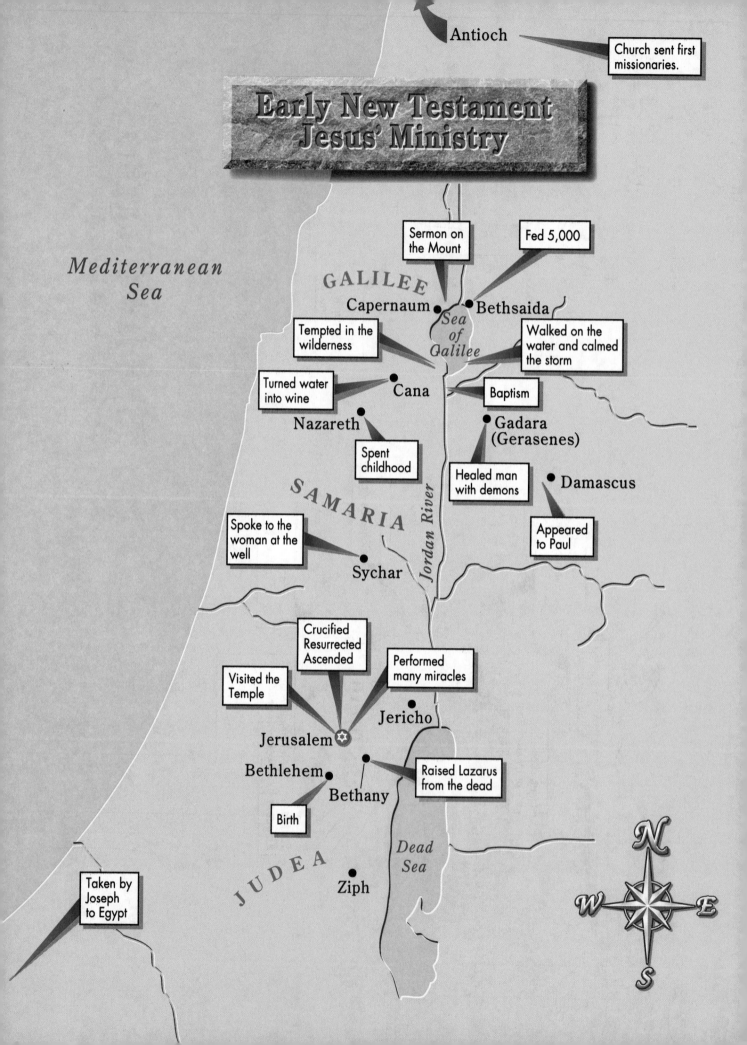